"No matter what child may face, no matter what grades he may bring home, no matter what his teachers may say, if you and your child talk openly, and work together to find solutions, and are secure in your parent/child relationship, your child is sure to find his optimal level of achievement in school."

—from the Preface

The premise of this book—that kids need their parents' help to do well in school—is a well-known fact. Now a renowned child psychologist and a seasoned schoolteacher, both parents themselves, give other parents the guidance they need to create the best possible learning environment for their children—paving the way for success both in school and in life.

CHARLES E. SCHAEFER, Ph.D., is a clinical professor of psychology at Fairleigh Dickinson University. Formerly director of psychological services at Children's Village in Dobbs Ferry, NY, he is a parent and the author of some twenty books, including *How to Help Children with Common Problems, Teach Your Baby to Sleep Through the Night,* and *Toilet Training Without Tears,* all available in Signet editions.

THERESA FOY DiGERONIMO, M.Ed., is a mother, writer, and former schoolteacher. She is the author of *Preemies: Caring for Premature Babies* and *AIDS: Trading Fears for Facts.* Schaefer and DiGeronimo are coauthors of *Teach Your Child to Behave,* which is available in an NAL Books edition.

Help Your Child Get the Most Out of School

Charles E. Schaefer, Ph.D.,
and
Theresa Foy DiGeronimo, M.Ed.

A PLUME BOOK

PLUME
Published by the Penguin Group
Penguin Books USA Inc., 375 Hudson Street, New York, New York 10014, U.S.A.
Penguin Books Ltd, 27 Wrights Lane, London W8 5TZ, England
Penguin Books Australia Ltd, Ringwood, Victoria, Australia
Penguin Books Canada Ltd, 2801 John Street, Markham, Ontario, Canada L3R 1B4
Penguin Books (N.Z.) Ltd, 182-190 Wairau Road, Auckland 10, New Zealand

Penguin Books Ltd, Registered Offices: Harmondsworth, Middlesex, England

First published by Plume, an imprint of New American Library,
a division of Penguin Books USA Inc.

First Printing, September, 1990
10 9 8 7 6 5 4 3 2 1

REGISTERED TRADEMARK—MARCA REGISTRADA

LIBRARY OF CONGRESS CATALOGING IN PUBLICATION DATA

Schaefer, Charles E.
    Help your child get the most out of school / by Charles E.
Schaefer and Theresa Foy DiGeronimo.
        p.   cm.
    Includes bibliographical references.
    ISBN 0-452-26499-5
    1. Education—Parent participation.   2. Home and school.
3. Parenting.   4. Study, Method of.   I. DiGeronimo, Theresa Foy.
II. Title.
LC225.S3225   1990
649′.68—dc20   90-36347
                                                        CIP

Printed in the United States of America
Set in Times Roman
Designed by Julian Hamer

BOOKS ARE AVAILABLE AT QUANTITY DISCOUNTS WHEN USED TO PROMOTE PRODUCTS OR SERVICES.
FOR INFORMATION PLEASE WRITE TO PREMIUM MARKETING DIVISION, PENGUIN BOOKS USA INC., 375
HUDSON STREET, NEW YORK, NEW YORK 10014.

Chart in Chapter 2 reproduced by special permission of the publisher, Consulting
Psychologists Press, Inc., Palo Alto, CA 94306, from *A Guide to Type: A New
Perspective on Individual Differences in the Classroom*, by Charles Meisgeier, Connie
Meisgeier, and Elizabeth Murphy © 1989. Further reproduction is prohibited without the
publisher's consent.

Quiz in Chapter 10 used by permission of the author, Michael K. Meyerhoff © 1988.

To our parents:
William and Loretta Schaefer
and
Joseph and Marilyn (Peggy) Foy,
who always recognized that education
is a family affair

Contents

ACKNOWLEDGMENTS

We would like to acknowledge the help of the following people:

Faith Hornby Hamlin, our agent, and Alexia Dorszynski, our Plume editor, for *always* supporting our efforts; the many children, parents, teachers, and administrators who gave us their time and their opinions—their input helped keep us focused on the aspects of education that are most important to parents; Dr. Joan Specht, Director of Special Programs in Hawthorne, New Jersey, for reviewing the chapter on special education; and Mrs. Lee Ann Hamilton, teacher of gifted and talented students, for reviewing the chapter on higher-level thinking skills and the information about education of gifted students.

A WORD ABOUT PRONOUNS

Both boys and girls need parental support and encouragement to reach their full academic potential. The information, advice, and suggested activities in this book apply equally to all children regardless of gender; however, in the interest of simplicity and uniformity we have decided to avoid the awkward and confusing reference to "he and she" and "him and her." Therefore, in this book all children are referred to as "he."

Help Your Child Get the Most Out of School

Introduction

Teachers alone are not capable of making your child reach his full academic potential. This statement isn't an indictment of teachers; it's a fact of child development. The premise of this book—that kids need their *parents'* help to do their best in school—is a well-known fact. Innumerable international, domestic, psychological, and educational studies have proven over and over again that the majority of children who reach an optimal level of academic achievement come from homes in which the parents set down the foundation for success. In such homes, the parents are involved in their children's schooling and work to build nurturing and supportive parent/child relationships.

Unfortunately, the logistics of building this foundation for school success can be difficult to manage. There are reams of information about the parent's role in education but too little time to take it all in, sort out what's practical from what's not, and then find ways to apply the useful information to your own children. That's why we have written this book. Knowing that most parents are juggling daily loads that leave little time for wading through the books and articles galore that offer how-to instruction on every aspect of a child's education, we have put in the time and the legwork to find what is best and immediately applicable. We've explored book stores and university, public, and school libraries, culling through volumes of research in books, pamphlets, booklets, articles, and curriculum guides. We have talked with parents and children, teachers, administrators, and school board members. We have combined our expertise and experiences in the fields of child psychology and education. And from all this we have pulled together what

1

we believe is a most psychologically and educationally sound program of parental involvement.

Each chapter in this book offers an overview of a specific area of education that parents have told us they are most concerned with. You can read this book from beginning to end and gain a solid understanding of your role in each aspect of your child's schooling, read only the chapters that are of most interest to you at the moment and come back to the others as you need them.

At the end of each chapter you will find a Resource List to give you other sources of information if you have the time and interest to delve more deeply. Some resource lists include available video cassettes and computer software programs that can be used to complement your efforts to help your child achieve in school. These supplemental aids have been recommended by elementary-school teachers who have used them and found them helpful. We are sure, however, that there is a wide variety of quality cassettes and software programs that we have not included. If you have a VCR and/or computer, read over our lists and ask your child's teacher to recommend additional cassettes and disks. Then check their availability at your local library and video rental store. If you cannot borrow these items first, ask the store owner for a chance to preview the programs. Since these video cassettes and computer software programs generally cost between twenty and one hundred dollars each, you'll want to be sure that they are appropriate for your child's age and needs before you buy.

As your child advances through his elementary-school years, his needs and thus your questions will continually change; it is our hope that throughout these years this book will remain a constant source of information. If the pages become worn and tattered we will have met our goal:

To help provide you with a practical tool that continually helps you enhance your child's ability to learn. But as you read, you must remember that no parent, not even a superparent, can implement all the suggestions in this book at once. So please don't try. Instead, focus on one specific area in which you would like to help your child improve, and then pull out of that chapter the activities and pieces of advice that you can most often and most confidently use.

Once you are comfortably using these on a regular basis, move on to another area. Don't hesitate to change your approach and try other suggested activities and strategies as your child grows.

As you incorporate these tactics and parenting skills into your family life, you will find one consistent message: No matter what school problems your child may face, no matter what grades he may bring home, no matter what his teachers may say, if the two of you talk openly, and work together to find solutions, and are secure in your parent/child relationship, your child is sure to find his optimal level of achievement in school.

1

"Are the schools doing a good job?"

A Parent's Role in Education

It's 8:15 P.M. on Elmwood Drive. The family scene in the Thompsons' home is typical of any weeknight at this time. The TV is turned off, and the evening newspaper lies open on the coffee table in the living room. George is sitting at the kitchen table with his 10-year-old son, Jimmy. They're going over today's school papers, and George is quizzing Jimmy on his spelling homework. Claire and 6-year-old Sara are sitting on the couch in the living room reading a book. As Claire reads the story, Sara picks out all the words she knows how to read. When the clock ticks to 8:30, Claire closes the book, Jimmy puts his papers away, and it's off to bed. As George helps Jimmy lay out his clothes for the next morning, he asks him what new things he might learn in school the next day. In the next room, despite Sara's pleas for just "one more TV show," Claire tucks her daughter in and reminds her to ask her teacher when the next PTA meeting will be. This scenario may sound like an idyllic scene from a 1950s TV sitcom, but actually the entire routine takes only 15 minutes every night, and it plays a vital role in helping the children reach their full academic potential.

The Johnson family lives across the street. Kathy and Hank love their children, and like their neighbors, they too work hard every day to make sure their children have everything they need. It is now 10:00 P.M. Hank is watching TV in the living room; Kathy is folding laundry in the kitchen; 10-year-old Timmy is playing a video game in his bedroom, and 6-year-old Jenny is asleep on the couch. For the fifth time, Hank yells to Timmy: "Turn that thing off and go to bed." For the fifth time, Timmy answers, "Okay." Kathy

4

adds (for the first time), "did you and your sister do your homework?" "Yeah," says Timmy. Without realizing it, Hank and Kathy are setting up attitudes, habits, and routines that can limit their children's ability to do well in school.

A Nation in Crisis

Both the Thompsons and the Johnsons have the right to expect the school system to give their children what they will need to become educated and productive adults. Unfortunately, the Johnsons, along with many other families and politicians, feel that the schools are not doing a good job. They point to children like Timmy and Jenny, who lack motivation and fail to achieve, as well as to studies and statistics that show a decline in standardized test scores, a decline in basic literacy and computation skills, an increase in poor attendance records and dropout rates, and a knowledge deficit that puts the United States far behind many Asian and European countries. They point with alarm to the headlines that publicized a 1983 federal report called "A Nation at Risk: The Imperative for Educational Reform," which found gapping holes in the American educational system.

This perceived crisis in education has given rise to the cry "What can be done to save our schools?" and a call for sweeping educational reforms in response. Prodded by their constituents, many state officials are asking for higher standards in teacher education programs, more accountability from school administrators, better school buildings and materials, and more government money to oversee the rehabilitation of a system in distress. These things, along with George Bush's commitment to be the "education president," may indeed help to improve the quality of American education; unfortunately however, the real crisis will not be addressed by fixing up the schools.

The Thompsons feel that the schools are doing a good job. Their children are motivated; they get along well with their teachers, and they get good grades. Perhaps the Thompsons are satisfied with the school system and their children's progress because they know something that is often overlooked by other families, the media, and politicians. Perhaps they read the concluding recommendations to *parents* in "A Nation at Risk," which stated:

". . . Your right to a proper education for your children carries a double responsibility. . . . your child's ideas about education and its significance begin with *you. You* must be a living example of what you expect your child to honor and to emulate. Moreover, *you* have a responsibility to participate actively in your child's education" (italics ours).[1]

Parents as Teachers

We parents have more influence on our children's education than any other single factor or combination of factors—bar none. This belief is supported by two decades of international studies in which educational researchers in twenty-one nations engaged in a cooperative examination of learning, teaching, and curriculum in their schools. They also compared their countries in terms of the achievement, interest, and attitudes of the students. These studies found great differences in every area of education, from curriculum to teacher competency, to the time spent teaching basic skills. However, in every analysis of the data, the one major factor that explains the differences in student performance is the *home environment.*[2]

This study, along with no less than forty-nine recent American studies, shares a conclusion: Parents create a curriculum and teaching style that account for most of the differences in a child's ability to do well in school. Also, parental involvement is consistently associated with higher grades, improved standardized achievement test scores, and teacher-rated competence as a learner—*regardless* of the child's I.Q.

What this says is that the schools alone are not responsible for the education of your child. Education does not happen exclusively between the hours of 9 and 3, approximately 180 days each year; instead, it is an on-going process that begins at birth and extends on through a lifetime. It is a process that has been found over and over again to work best when the school and home work together. The fact that you're reading this book indicates that you recognize the truth of this but have some unanswered questions about how to do it.

First, you should know the factors that have *nothing* to do with positive parental influence on education, which include your education, occupation, social class, socioeconomic status, race, or ethnic background. Thirty-seven years ago, a comprehensive study found that it is what parents *do* rather than what they *are* that accounts for the learning development of children.[3] You should also know that parents can go overboard and pressure children too much. Cramming facts into a child's head, supplementing school work with personal workbooks and drill sheets, and making him forfeit playtime for more school-work time is *not* the way to help your child succeed in school. Edward Zigler, former director of the Office of Child Development, says, "Over-emphasis on training the mind has led to a distorted view of parental tasks."[4]

As Zigler points out, helping a child learn can have positive consequences, but it can become harmful if it takes time and energy away from what parents uniquely have to offer their children: affectionate and personal attention. It is your job to foster optimal learning conditions by making your children feel loved and admired as individuals. This will give them the confidence they need to take advantage of the learning opportunities around them. The following are ways to establish a home environment that will enable your children to reach their full academic potential. The information in subsequent chapters will build upon this foundation.

Establish a Positive Relationship with Your Child

Before you look for ways you can help your child with his school work, look at the way the two of you relate to each other. Studies have shown that children learn best when they feel that their parents love, understand, and respect them. This kind of family bond doesn't just happen, however; it has to be nurtured with affection, self-sacrifice, and individualized attention. This is true no matter what combination of people make up your "family." The quality of your parent/child relationship will dictate the success of your efforts to help your child reach his full academic potential whether your family is of the traditional mom/dad/children type, or whether it consists of a single parent and children; a mom or dad, a lover, and children; or the weekend-visitation-type family. Whatever form your family takes, you will be able to motivate your child to do well in school *only* if he feels you are both on the same team working toward the same goal.

The best way to do this is to get to really know your child. Find out all you can about his likes and dislikes. What things are important to him? What things are difficult for him? If you are curious about your child and learn all you can about his opinions, beliefs, and experiences, you will find it easier to support and encourage his academic efforts. The following quiz, adapted from our book, *Teach Your Child to Behave*,[5] will help you determine how much you already know. After you have completed the form, ask your child for his answers and compare them with yours. This will let you know how much you really know about your child.

HOW WELL DO YOU KNOW YOUR CHILD?

	Parent's Response	Child's Response
1. What is your child's favorite color?		
2. What is your child most afraid of?		
3. Which teacher (past and present) has your child liked the most?		
4. What does your child want to be when he grows up?		
5. What book has your child enjoyed reading the most?		
6. If your child could change one thing about himself, what would it be?		

Parent's   Child's
Response   Response

7. What is your child's earliest memory? *Accide* _____

8. If your child could have one wish, what *move to Florida*
   would it be?   _____ _____

How did you do? If more than half your answers don't agree with your child's, you probably need to pay more attention to him in order to influence his academic achievements.

Set a Good Example

Once you have established a positive, affectionate relationship with your child, you will find that he is more likely to imitate your behavior, and follow your suggestions. Therefore, what you do and say will have great impact on your child's classroom performance each day.

Model an attitude of enthusiasm and excitement toward learning. Let your children see you tackle challenging projects (be it planting a garden, painting the porch, or rearranging furniture) with a positive attitude. Show them that you enjoy reading and learning new things. When you take your children to the library, borrow books for yourself. When your child sits down to do homework, take out your "homework" of bills, letters, reading, etc., and proceed with good humor and confidence. If you have the time and opportunity, take an adult course in something. Let your child see that learning is a lifelong endeavor. You might make this point by occasionally steering conversations back to your own school days. Tie in what you're doing now (measuring lumber for the backyard deck, preparing a tax form, or brushing up on your French as you pack for a vacation on the Riviera) to what you learned in school. A simple statement such as "I'm glad my fourth grade teacher made me memorize all those grammar rules or I'd never be able to write this newsletter for my boss" will help your child see a relationship between what he does in school and what he'll need in life. Child experts agree that children who observe their parents' positive attitude toward learning are more likely to "catch" the feeling and apply it to their own school work. Remember—children learn more from a model than from a critic.

Foster Language Development

Words are the tools your child uses for thinking and communicating. Therefore, he needs well-developed language skills to do his best in school. Because children learn language skills by listening to others speak, you have a daily opportunity to give your child an advantage by setting a good example in your own speech patterns and by making a concerted effort to emphasize language development in your home.

Model good language habits. When you talk, make sure you're using the speech patterns you want your child to imitate. If, for example, you say to a friend, "I seen you at the store last week," your child will imitate your mistakes in his own speech and then in his writing as well. Take care to speak naturally and clearly when you talk to your child. Encourage him to talk to you and to tell you stories. (Don't nag or interrupt him while he's talking.) Give him your attention so that he learns that what he has to say has value. If your child is a chatterbox, you certainly don't need to encourage him to talk. But you may find it impossible to give him your full attention every time he wants to tell a story. In this case, explain to your child that although he's welcome to keep talking, you have to do other things while you listen; then, when your work is finished, find at least 15 minutes to sit down and give him your full attention.

Of course most parents already spend at least 15 minutes talking with their children each day. But when you talk, take some time to listen to what you're saying. It would not be unusual if 99 percent of your "conversations" sounded like this:

Parent: "Hurry up and eat breakfast or you'll be late for school."

Parent: "Don't kick your sister's feet under the table."

Parent: "Will you watch what you're doing; your milk is spilling all over the place."
Parent: "Don't forget your lunch."
Parent: "When you leave don't slam the door behind you."

The most obvious flaw in these "conversations" is the lack of interaction. In many homes, parents talk, children listen (or pretend to listen). On busy schedules it is difficult to spend time each day actually talking *with* your child, but it can be done if you make the effort. Use the time you spend running errands, traveling back and forth from school, and doing household jobs to engage your child in actual back-and-forth conversation. Fortunately for busy parents, almost everything in the day-to-day environment can be used to encourage language development.

At first you may find your conversations will follow a pattern similar to the following:

Parent: "How was school today?"
Child: "Okay."
Parent: "Was there anything new happening?"
Child: "No."
Parent: "Is there anything you want to talk about?"
Child: "No."

If this happens, don't assume that your child doesn't want to talk to you. Make your questions more specific: "What did you do in gym class today?" "How is your substitute teacher different from your regular teacher?" "How is your friend doing in math class this year?"

In addition to encouraging your child to discuss his day with you, try some of the following word games suggested by Academic Therapy Publications.[6] They will show your child that vocabulary development is not only the memorization of word lists in school, but can involve activities that are fun for the whole family.

- If your child has started formal spelling at school, post the word list on the refrigerator door. Use those words with your child as discussions arise, and encourage him to use them in his responses.

- Start a subscription to a child's magazine. There are many of these, and they cover practically every interest area of children—cars, sports, computers, the out-of-doors, etc.
- Think up ways of building on your child's special interest or hobby. For example, a scrapbook is fun to make and keep and will help to build vocabulary skills if contents are carefully labeled and described.
- If distant family members have cassette players, send "letters" on tape. After each family member has his or her say, mail it out and ask the relative to record a message and send it back.
- Play homonym games. Ask family members to hunt for words that sound alike but are spelled differently and mean something different, such as "sun" and "son." Then post the growing list on the refrigerator and encourage your child to add to it each day. There are numerous homonyms in our language and your list may well include: "rain," "rein," and "reign," "flour" and "flower," and "night" and "knight."
- Word Origins of or facts about words can be fascinating family fare. For example, the word "salary" had its origin in *salarium*, which is Latin for salt. Roman soldiers received their pay in salt. Ask your librarian to help you find books that will provide other interesting examples of the origin of common words.

Establish a Daily Routine and Positive Work Habits

Most often school classrooms are structured work environments; children are expected to perform certain tasks within a given unit of time and then to move on to the next task. The ease with which your child can apply himself to his reading lessons, finish the assignment, and be mentally ready to move on to math lessons depends on the kind of daily routine and work habits he picks up at home.

You can enhance your child's ability to do well in school by establishing a predictable routine in your home. Children gain a sense of security and self-control when they know what time they will wake up, what time they will have dinner, how long they can play, when it's time to do homework, and when it's time for bed. On the other hand, children who go from day to day without knowing what to expect or how to budget their time and to organize their play and work schedules may develop a sense of disorganization and helplessness. These feelings can keep them from achieving daily goals because the goals seem unclear or out of their control.[7]

Also, children who live with unpredictable schedules may not achieve daily goals because they simply run out of time. The time needed to do homework, special projects, and daily reading can be easily gobbled up by too much playtime and TV viewing time. For children without a schedule, bedtime comes suddenly (or the child falls asleep on the couch while watching TV). Children need a good night's sleep; they need playtime and TV time, but they also need a set time for doing their school work. Within an established routine, you and your child will find that there is time for all of these things.

Your child's attitude toward his school work will also affect how well he gets the job done. For good or ill, your child will pick up his attitude toward work directly from you. How do you talk about your job? Do you set challenging standards and show pride of accomplishment when the work is done? Or do you complain and look for shortcuts that will let you do the job quickly and without effort in order to have it over with? Whether you're a homemaker, a carpenter, or the chairman of the executive board, listen to yourself when you talk about your work. Make sure that what you say is what you want your child to imitate.

The work habits that your child practices at home while doing his chores affect the way he approaches his school work. Your child probably has some job that he must do around the house, whether cleaning up his toys each night, or taking out the garbage, or setting the table, or feeding the dog. Whatever the job, use it to teach your child strong, positive work habits.

First, explain to your child *exactly* what you expect. Don't give vague instructions like, "I want you to clean your room." Say specifically, "Every night at 8:00, I want you to put all your clothes, books, and toys in your bedroom where they belong."

Secondly, check to be sure the work is done, and done properly, every night. This will let your child know that you want him to take this job seriously. Very often it's much easier and faster to let disobedience slide, or to do the job yourself, but if you do this, you're depriving your child of the opportunity to learn responsible work habits.

Children need to learn that half-hearted efforts aren't acceptable and that "forgetting" is never an excuse. They also need to feel the satisfaction that comes with a job done well. If you want your child to do his school work in a responsible and whole-hearted manner, give him opportunities at home to develop that kind of positive work ethic.

Nurture a Sense of Competence

What makes *you* feel competent? Most people have this feeling when they accomplish something challenging and feel they can do it again in the future. If your child develops a sense of competence he is likely to do better in school than students without it—even if those other students are more intelligent—because people tend to take on challenging work that they feel they are capable of handling. In the same way, they tend to avoid activities and situations they feel are beyond their capabilities.[8]

Maryann and Lynn, for example, both have to make a science project that demonstrates their knowledge of the solar system. Their sense of competence will dictate how well each handles the assignment. Maryann, who has an average IQ, listened to her teacher explain the assignment and immediately assured herself, "I can do that. I can make a terrific project that will show where all the planets are found in the solar system." At home that night, Maryann went right to work—mapping out her project, trying out several ideas, gathering together materials, and sharing her plans with her family. Because it never occurred to Maryann that she couldn't do this project, she was willing to spend time and effort on it and then persist when faced with obstacles. Lynn, on the other hand, who is of above-average intelligence, listened to the details of the assignment with the feeling, "Oh, no. I can't do this. Everyone will laugh at what I make; it'll probably fall apart; I can't think of anything special." So she put off even thinking about this project, didn't mention it to her family for fear they'd start to nag her to get going on it, and was unwilling to exert effort or to persevere through the problems of planning, creating, and presenting her ideas. Since Lynn didn't believe she could do a good job, she didn't feel it was worth putting in the time or effort. Obviously, in school, at work, and in life, a person with a strong sense of competency will achieve a greater degree of success.

You can nurture a sense of competence in your child by creating opportunities for success. When your child attempts something new—flying a kite, or caring for his new pet, or building a model airplane—encourage and praise the effort. Hold back critical comments like, "Not like that!" Or, "You're doing it all wrong." Or, "You're making a mess of that." The first clumsy attempts to master new skills will teach your child how to face obstacles, try again, and relish the feelings of satisfaction that come when a challenging task is mastered. If your child asks for help, give it freely. But remember to give it with support and encouragement, rather than with statements like, "I knew you couldn't do this yourself." When your child wants to take on a challenge, send him off with the feeling that "if this can be done, I certainly can do it."

Children need to experience success to gain a sense of mastery, but they also need to experience occasional failure. Children who experience only easy successes come to expect quick results and their sense of competency is easily replaced with self-doubt when they experience failure. Setbacks and difficulties serve a useful purpose—teaching that success usually requires sustained effort. When a child persists in his efforts to achieve and eventually is rewarded with success, he learns that life's failures, adversities, setbacks, frustrations, and inequities are no reason to lose faith in his capabilities. They are reasons to attack the problem with renewed vigor, knowing that eventually a route to success will be found.

You can further nurture this sense of competency by giving your child freedom to explore. To do this you'll need to develop a high tolerance for mistakes and accept them as a method of learning. Lynn may have decided that she couldn't do the solar system project because she was afraid of doing it "wrong." If that was the case her sense of competency has been undermined by a belief that whatever she does must be done the "right" way. Maryann, however, was willing to try one approach and if it didn't work try another and another until she was satisfied. Of course, her parents could have told her from the start which approach would work best, but instead they supported Maryann's need to try it "my way." They helped her see errors and mistakes as learning experiences rather than failures. This tolerant attitude allows Maryann to attempt creative solutions without fear of ridicule or "failure." It lets her satisfy her "what if . . ." kind of curiosity without worrying that she'll appear silly. By giving her the freedom to make mistakes, Maryann's parents have helped her develop a strong sense of competency.

Once your child adopts an "I-can-do-it" attitude, help him maintain that feeling. He can do this by using positive mental rehearsals. Several studies have found that when individuals visualize themselves skillfully executing activities they actually do enhance their performance.[9] Before he presents his oral book report, for example, encourage your child to imagine himself going through the process of giving the report confidently and successfully. This will help him feel confident when it's actually time to do it. Encourage your child to talk about his feelings toward challenging assignments. If he shows a lack of competence by envisioning things going wrong, help him replace those negative thoughts with positive ones. The negative thoughts will undermine his performance and reinforce the chain of failure, which weakens a child's sense of competence and which in turn promotes the possibility of another failure.

Be Involved

Most children cannot maintain their interest and commitment to the learning process unless they get support and encouragement from home. You can do this best by being an active parent. Find out what your child is learning in each subject area. Watch closely for trouble areas by talking to his teacher on a regular basis, reading over his notebooks and homework assignments, and helping him study for tests. This will tell you where you can offer needed help and encouragement. (See Chapter 8 for more detailed information about how to develop a positive parent/child/teacher relationship.) This kind of active parenting means *doing*. Instead of saying, "I encourage my child to visit the library once a week," active parents say, "I take my child to the library once a week." Rather than saying, "I want my child to read for a half-hour every night," try *doing*: "I read to (or with) my child for one half-hour every night." Don't wait for problems to come home to you. Stay involved in your child's work to actively prevent them.

Monitoring your child's school lessons also gives you an opportunity to notice areas you can praise and draw attention to. Display his papers on the refrigerator. Tell your friends and neighbors (within earshot of your child) about his special accomplishments. Give him special rewards for special achievements. (See Chapter 4 for more details on rewarding school work.) Positive attention is a great motivator!

You can also stay involved in your child's education by keeping tabs on his daily routines at home. Make sure that he studies for tests and completes projects on time and that he has an established homework schedule. (See Chapter 5 for complete details on how to do this.) Also, keep track of your child's school attendance record. If you find that he is missing more than three days of school each month because of vague "I-don't-feel-so-good" complaints, take him to your pediatrician, school physician, or nurse for a physical exam. If he's in good health, implement the motivational strategies suggested in Chapter 4 and insist that he go to school. When he goes to school, make sure he is well rested and fed. Children need energy to remain physically and mentally alert in school, if they are tired and hungry they will not be able to do their best work.

Create an Environment for Learning

Create an atmosphere in your home that will help your child see education as a positive and natural part of his life. Speak highly about your child's school and teachers in daily conversations. Occasionally mention the value of education in the job market and in improving the quality of one's life. This will pass on to your child an attitude of respect for his place of learning.

You can make your home reflect this attitude by making reading materials and study resources readily available. Bring newspapers and magazines into your home; encourage your child to read them (or read them to him if he's very young), and bring the headlines into your dinner conversations. Keep study aids handy and encourage your child to read and investigate:

- Get a *dictionary* that's appropriate to your child's level of understanding. Encourage him to pay attention to new words and to get into the "dictionary habit."
- Let your child navigate by using *maps* during trips around town. Plan a route beforehand and teach your child how to follow it on a map.
- Use the *encyclopedia* to locate and read about countries and facts mentioned in the news or in class lessons.

In today's computer age you may wonder if a personal computer is a necessary home learning aid. The answer is, No. Computers are used in 86 percent of our public and private schools because children do need to learn how to use computers to keep pace with the use of technology in today's world. There are also some software programs that help to reinforce classroom lessons. But in the home, elementary-school-age students need personal, attentive parental support and opportunities for hands-on, active learning. Academic success is rarely achieved by sitting alone at an electronic keyboard answering rigid right or wrong questions. And unfortunately, the computer sometimes offers parents one more way to become *un*involved in their child's education.

If you already have a computer in your home, use it wisely. Sit down *with* your child and explore electronic academics together. Choose software carefully to ensure that you aren't giving your child material that is either too easy or too challenging. Using the computer *with* your child will enhance your child's education simply by virtue of the fact that it brings the two of you together to explore another mode of learning. When your child moves on to high school and college, a home computer may indeed be an asset (if not a necessity). But for now, you will probably do more to enhance your child's chances of achieving academic success by structuring a supportive home environment than by buying a computer.

You can also enhance the atmosphere of learning in your home by using the TV to its fullest educational advantage. Since 88.6 million American households have at least one television set, it's a good bet that there's one in your home. It's another good bet that you've sometimes wondered if the amount of TV viewing allowed in your home is good, bad, or indifferent in its effect on your child's success in school. Most child-development experts feel that a turned-on television set is not in itself bad for your child; television use is as good or as bad as you allow it to be.

"Bad" TV use is indiscriminate use. If your child (or you) is in the habit of plopping down in front of the TV to watch hours of whatever happens to appear on the screen, he is forfeiting time that could be better spent playing with friends, reading books, getting fresh air and exercise, or daydreaming. The Nielsen report says 6- to 11-year-olds watch TV on an average of 22 hours each week—and most of the programs viewed during this time are inappropriate for the child's age and offer a distorted view of his world.

"Good" TV use is carefully monitored use. It can take your child from underwater expeditions to a walk on the moon, from presidential inaugurations to tribal celebrations in South Africa. You have absolute control over the effect TV use will have on your child. *Exercise* that control and by personally selecting which shows your child can watch and by limiting the number of hours allowed for viewing each day. (We don't pretend that your child won't complain loudly and watch "bad" TV at his friends' homes. But monitoring your child's TV-watching habits certainly will reduce the negative effects and enhance the kind of home atmosphere that improves school performance.) Watch the selected shows with your child, or at least keep an ear tuned in. This way you can be sure that the show is giving your child information and social views that are in line with what you would teach him yourself. You can then use the TV show as a base for family discussion. Ask your child if he agrees with the decision the TV character made. Ask him what he would do in that situation. Ask him if he thinks people in real life act like the ones on TV. Ask him to talk about what he watches.

If you're among the 50 percent of Americans who own a VCR, you can have even greater control over what your child watches on TV. You can carefully select and preview shows that will provide "good" viewing. You can tape shows that are on TV late at night or during the school day for viewing after school. You can also record programs of particular interest or value and keep them for "re-run" showing.

TV can assist you in your efforts to help your child do well in school, or it can sabotage them. Sit down and talk with your child about TV viewing; together, create a weekly schedule that balances his favorite shows with educational ones. Teach him how to choose shows that will expand—not close—his mind.

Creating a supportive home environment takes time and planning. But once the positive attitudes toward learning are established, the study resources are in place, and the TV rules are habit, you'll find your efforts will be repaid in the achievements of your children.

Set High Standards and Expectations

Children need to know what their parents expect them to achieve. When the message from home says "reach high and always give your best," the child himself will come to believe that haphazard, sloppy, and incomplete work is not acceptable. This doesn't mean that all parents should say to their children, "You must get A's on your tests." It *does* mean that parents who are involved in their child's school work and who know his capabilities, limitations, and talents can set standards of excellence that challenge the child to exert his best effort.

We can learn a lesson from the Japanese and Chinese when it comes to setting high standards and clear expectations. A recent study by Dr. H. W. Stevenson at the University of Michigan asked mothers from Japan, Taiwan, and America what they thought most influenced student achievement. The American mothers said, "talent and native ability." The Asian mother emphasized "hard work and effort."[10] This is an important difference, because if parents believe that natural ability is the principal source of achievement, they don't have to nurture it by paying attention to the curriculum, or by monitoring TV time, or by being supportive or encouraging. But if parents believe that effort is the key to success, then they are much more likely to be closely involved in the educational process and to set high standards of achievement. In Japan, parents and teachers expect a consistently high level of academic performance from the students. They assume that with hard work and perseverance, most children can master school work—even though it may come easier to the more gifted students. The Japanese simply refuse to concede that a child's aptitude, interests, or even family finances offer an excuse for poor school performance.

Give your child a consistent message that all-out effort is the norm in your house. Then encourage him to aspire to higher levels of education and vocation. Help him make plans for high school and college and then help him see his present school lessons in relation to these future goals.

In sum, the attitudes toward education that children bring into the classroom come from their home. If they feel that learning is unimportant and a waste of time, their chances of reaching their full academic potential are slim. If, on the other hand, they feel that learning and effort are necessary, worthwhile, and exciting, there is no telling how far they will go. Because you have more influence on your child than anyone else, rise to the challenge to foster a love of learning—then you, with your schools, can insure that he receives a quality A + education.

Resource List

Write

- Action for Children's Television (ACT)
  20 University Road
  Cambridge, Massachusetts 02138
  Send self-addressed, stamped envelope for details.
- Home and School Institute
  Special Project Office
  1201 16th St. N.W.
  Washington, D.C. 20036
  1-202-466-3633.
  This institute offers a wide variety of academic and social development materials for families to use with children.
- Parents' Choice
  Box 185
  Newton, Massachusetts 02168
  This foundation publishes a quarterly newsletter reviewing children's television, videos, books, toys, and other media. A one-year subscription is $15.00.
- The Office of Educational Research and Improvement
  U.S. Department of Education
  Washington, D.C. 20208
  This government office publishes several very practical "Help Your Child" pamphlets.
- The National PTA
  700 N. Rush St.
  Chicago, Illinois 60611
  Send 10 cents for a copy of the pamphlet "Help Your Young Child Learn at Home."

- The National Committee for Citizens in Education (NCCE)
  10840 Little Patuxent Parkway, Suite 301
  Columbia, MD 21044
  This committee helps parents resolve problems with schools.
  For advice on a specific problem or concern, call toll free:
  1-800-NET-WORK.

Books

- *Getting the Most Out of TV*
  Singer, Singer, and Zuckerman
  Good Year Books, 1981
- *Help Your Child in School*
  Bernard Percy
  Prentice-Hall, 1980
- *How to Help Your Child Succeed in School*
  William and Susan Stainback
  Meadowbrook, 1988
- *Parent Power*
  Sherry Ferguson and Lawrence Mazin
  Clarkson N. Potter, Inc., 1989
- *The School Smart Parent*
  Gene I. Maeroff
  Times Books, 1989
- *The TV-Smart Book for Kids*
  Peggy Charren and Carol Hulsizer
  E.P. Dutton, 1986

Video Cassette

- *Everything You Always Wanted to Know About Computers*
  MGM (catalog #400460) VHS and Beta
  This is a simple guide to home computers including "How
  to Choose a Computer"; "Software"; and "Do's and
  Don't's."

Computer Software

- *Dictionary Skills*
  Random House Media (1-800-638-6460)
  Grade levels: 3rd to 6th grade
  Apple
  Gives practice in placing vocabulary words in alphabetical order.
- *Vocabulary Development*
  Weekly Reader Software (1-800-327-1473)
  Grade levels: 3rd to 6th grade
  Apple and IBM
  Helps children learn new words.

2

"Is this the best you can do?"

Determining and Using Information About Your Child's IQ, Personality Type, and Learning Style

Greg is a perfectionist; Jennifer is inattentive; Alex is very organized; Kate is "gifted"; and John has been labeled a "difficult" child. All of these 11-year-olds are in the same classroom, learning the same lessons from the same teacher. Most likely they will all be expected to act, respond, and learn in the same manner. Unfortunately, that won't happen, because each is a different kind of person. Although personal characteristics are often overlooked or ignored in crowded classrooms, you can enhance your child's school experience by learning how IQ, personality type, and learning style affect academic performance.

Intelligence Quotient (IQ)

Your child has an intelligence quotient (IQ) that can be used to predict how well he will do in school. It is generally believed, for example, that if a child has a very high IQ, he will be at or near the top of the class, while a child with a low score will struggle to keep up with his classmates. This information can be used constructively to set appropriate standards and expectations for children, but because of its limitations, an IQ score can also be misunderstood or misused. Let's take a look at the facts.

History of IQ Tests

The IQ test as we know it today was "invented" almost a century ago by a French psychologist, Alfred Binet. The Ministry of Education had asked Binet to devise a way of identifying children who were not likely to benefit from the typical school environment because of what was called "feeblemindedness." Binet then later revised his test of feeblemindedness to predict different levels of school success. (It is a bit ironic that the test that now is most often used to identify gifted children was first intended to identify "feebleminded" ones.) In 1916 the test was again modified by Lewis Terman of Stanford University. This American version, called the Stanford-Binet, along with intelligence tests devised by psychologist David Wechsler, are today the most commonly used measure of academic "intelligence."

Kind of Test

A standard intelligence test is an aptitude designed to predict a person's ability to learn and to do well in school. It is *not* meant to be an achievement test that measures specific learned information.

Sample Questions

The best way to explain what kind of intelligence the IQ test measures is to take a look at the type of questions on the test. The Wechsler Intelligence Scale for Children-Revised (WISC-R), for example, is composed of ten sections that take about one hour to complete. Five of the subtests ask for verbal responses, and five others analyze performance skills. Sample questions (which have been altered slightly to protect the security of the tests) include:

Verbal Scale:

1. *Information:* Where does rain come from?
2. *Similarities:* In what way are a train and a car alike?
3. *Arithmetic:* How many 50-cent toys can you buy with 3 dollars? (These questions must be answered within 45 seconds without the use of pencil or paper.)
4. *Vocabulary:* What is a "supermarket"?
5. *Comprehension:* What would you do if you fell down and cut your knee? (Such questions are intended to evaluate a child's judgment and common sense.)

Performance Scale:

1. *Picture Completion:* The child is asked to look at a line drawing and tell what part is missing.
2. *Picture Arrangement:* The child is asked to arrange a series of three to five pictures in logical sequence.
3. *Block Design:* The child is asked to reproduce a colored pattern of blocks in a given picture with actual blocks.
4. *Object Assembly:* A child puts together cut-up representations of a house, horse, tree, etc.
5. *Coding:* A child must comprehend symbol codes that are given to a group of numbers. He must then fill in blank boxes with the symbol representations of each number.

Scoring

Correct and quick responses to these ten categories of questions will produce a high IQ score. Therefore, the IQ score reflects the reasoning skills that are required to answer these kinds of questions. The results are scaled as follows:

Less than 80	=	Below average
Between 80 and 90	=	Low average
Between 90 and 110	=	Average
Between 110 and 120	=	High average
Over 120	=	Superior

Obtaining the Scores

If you want to know your child's IQ score, ask your school's principal if the scores are included in your child's student record. Although the test scores are not usually sent home to the parents, you have a right to this information if you request it. The availability of IQ scores is not usually openly advertised by school administrators because parents may wrongly use them to compare and label their children. However, if you recognize the limitations of IQ testing described on page 30, you can use your child's general range of IQ to set realistic expectations. This score can also help you determine if your child is either gifted, underachieving, or learning disabled and therefore in need of specialized modes of instruction. (See Chapter 10 for a discussion of special education.)

If IQ tests are not given in your child's school, you can arrange to have a test administered by a child psychologist. Call your state or county psychological association and ask for a referral to a child psychologist who specializes in cognitive assessment.

Raising the Score

Most parents (even those who don't know their child's IQ score) are anxious to know, "Can I raise my child's level of intelligence, or was he born with an IQ that remains constant throughout his life?" These questions are debatable and have spawned intensive and global research projects. Most studies now indicate that both heredity and environment play a role in affecting IQ. Your child is born with a certain degree of intelligence that can then be substantially affected by his environment.

Studies conducted at the Fels Research Institute in Yellow Springs, Ohio, show the average child changed 28.5 IQ points between 2½ and 17 years of age. Those children whose IQ scores increased tended to have parents who attempted to accelerate and encourage their intellectual growth and who provided firm but not authoritarian discipline. (See Chapter 4 for a full explanation of authoritarian discipline.) These studies also found that for unspecified reasons some children lost their intellectual advantage between the ages of 10 and 17.[1]

Given the fact that a child's IQ is not frozen on one rung of the intellectual ladder, the next question you might ask is, "How can I raise my child's IQ?" Some books and magazine articles would have you believe that you can significantly raise your child's IQ through rigorous academic programs. While it is true that you can influence your child's mental abilities, this is not effectively done by drilling with flash cards or spending hours cramming facts into your child's growing brain. You can readily affect intellectual development (as explained in Chapter 1) by creating a home environment and family attitude that encourage respect for learning and a curiosity about life. Overall, you can do this in these general ways:

- Make an effort to consistently expose your child to a variety of experiences—the circus, museums, art shows, town carnivals, etc.
- Answer his questions when you can ("How many seconds are in one minute?"), work together to find the answers when you can't ("How far is it to Mars?"), and encourage your child to answer his own questions when appropriate ("Why do I have to do homework?").
- Provide consistent support and encouragement for your child's academic, creative, and social ventures.
- Set an example as a person who is productively engaged in stimulating activities. A parent who sits around every evening watching hours of TV cannot hope to affect a child's intellectual potential.
- Encourage higher-level thinking skills such as observation, cause-and-effect reasoning, classification, comparison, inference, imagination, creativity, and problem-solving. (See Chapter 3 for a full discussion of these thinking skills.)
- Provide your child with a well-balanced diet and sleep schedule that will give him the physical and mental energy to become actively engaged in learning.

If you do these things in a consistent and nurturing manner, you will help your child perform in an optimal manner on IQ tests.

Limitations of IQ Test Scores

Knowing your child's IQ and knowing that you can influence its development can help you encourage your child's academic achievement. You should realize, however, that the IQ test has certain limitations, and therefore, the results can be misused. The most obvious limitation of an IQ score is that it is obtained in a testing situation. This leaves the results open to a number of factors that could alter the score; test anxiety, noises and distractions, the rapport between the child and the examiner, even the child's physical and emotional state at the time can easily affect motivation, interest, and intellectual fervor.

You must also remember that the IQ score can change. A school or family that labels a child as slow, for example, may be handing that child a lifelong sentence of failure since low expectations can negatively affect his self-image and motivation. Because this often happens, the federal government has made it illegal for schools to use IQ test scores as the sole means of assigning students to special education classes. Except in cases of mental retardation, low scores should not be used to diagnose a child; they should be used as motivation to find better ways to help him comprehend and respond to his school work.

Traditional IQ scores have a limited useful application. They have been fairly consistent in their ability to predict success in school but there appears to be little relationship between IQ and success in life. This may be due to the narrow aspect of "intelligence" tapped by these tests. Psychologists once believed that by combining the verbal, mathematical, and logical reasoning scores they could find a general mental ability—called "g." That idea is being challenged today by a growing number of developmentalists led by Harvard psychologist Dr. Howard Gardner. He believes that intelligence can be divided into numerous categories. In a recent interview in *Children* magazine, Gardner stated, "There's a tremendous temptation in our society to think of kids as being smart or stupid in schoolwork, and of that being the only dimension that counts."[2] These "other" dimensions are outlined in Dr. Gardner's book, *Frames of*

Mind (Basic Books, 1983).[3] In sum, he proposes seven kinds of intelligence:

1. *Linguistic intelligence,* which is characterized by a sensitivity to the meaning and order of words. (This kind of intelligence is used by writers, translators, and actors.)
2. *Logical-mathematical intelligence,* which is characterized by an ability in mathematics and other complex logical systems. (This is most often found in computer analysts, economists, and scientists.)
3. *Musical intelligence,* which is characterized by the ability to understand and create music. (All kinds of musicians and dancers utilize this intelligence.)
4. *Spatial intelligence,* which is found in people who "think in pictures." This involves the ability to perceive visual words accurately and recreate them in the mind or on paper. (Artists, architects, designers and sculptors display spatial intelligence.)
5. *Bodily-kinesthetic intelligence,* which is characterized by the use of one's body in a skilled way, for self-expression or toward a goal. (The mime, the dancer, the basketball player display bodily-kinesthetic intelligence.)
6. *Interpersonal intelligence,* characterized by an ability to perceive and understand other individuals—their moods, desires and motivations. (This intelligence is found in effective politicians, salespeople, and psychologists.)
7. *Intrapersonal intelligence* is characterized by an understanding of one's own emotions. (Writers, entrepreneurs, psychologists, and ministers use this skill to enable them to deal more effectively with others.)

By these definitions, then, a child who is failing in his academic work is not necessarily lacking in "intellect." In this case, our job as parents is to find the child's areas of strength and use them to improve his chances of success in life. (The following section will help you find those areas of strength and suggest learning styles and activities that emphasize what your child does best.)

Knowing the limitations of traditional IQ tests and the possibility of multiple intelligence types, you should be cautious about jumping on an IQ score and holding it up as either an excuse for poor school work or as a high mark that must be reflected in every aspect of life. IQ scores are no more than a singular and imperfect measure of your child's complete make-up. Regardless of the test score, your child is a unique and complex individual. Combining IQ with the following information about personality type and learning style will give you a fuller picture of your child's interests, capabilities, and needs.

Personality and Learning Style

Personality is the part of your child that gives him traits such as being strong-willed, or easily distracted, or persistent, or easy-going, or prone to perfectionism. In the elementary-school years, children display one of several different personality types. These types have been found to significantly influence the way a child learns. By recognizing your child's personality type, you will be better able to support the learning style that grows out of these traits and preferences.

In the early twentieth century, Swiss psychiatrist Carl Jung introduced the concept of psychological types. Today, the psychological types of adults are commonly identified through the Myers-Briggs Type Indicator® (MBTI®). The results of this test have been widely used in counseling, career planning, staff and professional development, education, and personal growth. Now an adapted scale—the Murphy-Meisgeier Type Indicator for Children® (MMTIC®)—can help you better understand, support, and guide your child through his school years. A thorough and accurate assessment of psychological type can be obtained from a professional who is trained in psychological assessment. But even without a professional analysis, you can use the following information about psychological types to gain some insight into the kinds of internal factors that are influencing your child's efforts to learn.

You can begin the hunt for your child's psychological type by asking yourself the following questions:

- Does your child focus on the inner world of thoughts and ideas, or on the outer world of people, events, and things?

- How does your child experience and learn about life and the world?
- How does your child make decisions about what he experiences and learns?
- Does your child strive for predictability and order, or is he more comfortable with flexibility and spontaneity?

The answers to these questions will help you begin to identify the individual differences that are called preferences. Most children's preferences will be found among the following eight types:

DEFINITIONS OF THE PREFERENCES

Where Attention Is Focused

Extraversion (E)

Children with a preference for Extraversion are stimulated by the people, things, and activities in their environment. They are sociable and enjoy active participation in tasks.

Introversion (I)

Children with a preference for Introversion are oriented toward the inner world and focus on ideas, concepts, and impressions. They enjoy privacy and work well alone or with just a few others.

How Information Is Received

Sensing (S)

Children with a preference for Sensing receive information directly through the five senses. Practical and realistic, they focus on what is going on around them in the present.

Intuition (N)

Children with a preference for Intuition perceive information through a "sixth sense." They tend to be imaginative and creative and focus on future possibilities.

How Judgments or Decisions Are Made

Thinking (T)

Children with a preference for Thinking make decisions based on logic. They try to remain objective when forming a judgment and are good at analyzing problems.

Feeling (F)

Children with a preference for Feeling make decisions on the basis of personal values. They are concerned about people and consider the impact of decisions on others.

How Children Orient to the Outer World

Judging (J)

Children with a preference for Judging take an orderly, planned approach to life. They like to organize activities, make decisions, and finish projects.

Perceiving (P)

Children with a preference for Perceiving take a spontaneous, flexible approach to life. They are curious and adaptable and prefer to stay open to new experiences.

Meisgeier, C., Meisgeier, C., and Murphy, E. (1989). *A Teacher's Guide to Type: A New Perspective on Individual Differences in the Classroom.* Palo Alto, CA: Consulting Psychologists Press, 1989, page 3.

According to type theory, each child will eventually develop and use all eight preferences, though they will not be equally preferred. Most children have a predisposition toward one of the preferences in each of the four categories. To identify your child's preferred psychological type, choose one preference from each of the four categories that best describe him and then record the corresponding letters that are in parentheses. If, for example, your child works best among people (E), takes in information concretely with his five senses (S), makes decisions in an objective logical way (T), and likes his world orderly and structured (J), his psychological type would read: ESTJ.

The value of knowing your child's psychological type lies in what you can do with it. For example, Paul's parents fought a nightly homework battle with him because they thought he should work alone in his room, that he should be able to grasp the concepts in a reading assignment after one silent reading, and that he should take responsibility himself for setting aside homework time. They changed their expectations, however, once they realized that Paul's psychological type included E (a preference for working with people), S (a preference for concrete facts over abstract concepts), T (a desire for logical presentation of information), and J (a need for an organized routine). Now they encourage him to study with a friend; they help him find concepts that can be derived from the facts of his assignments; they help him outline complex reading assignments; and they have arranged a set daily homework time. Paul's parents can now see that Paul had not been intentionally difficult about doing his homework; he was bucking a set of circumstances that worked against his natural inclinations.

The authors of *A Parent's Guide to Type: Individual Differences at Home and in School* remind parents that when children's activities do not actively engage their preference types, they are forced to use less preferred functions: "This is like asking naturally right-handed children continually to use their left hand: although they may develop some skill in writing this way, their performance may be far below potential and learning may be stressful."[4] With this in mind, you can see why it is believed that misunderstood personality type may account for many of the difficulties children experience at home and in school.

The following information about psychological types is taken from *A Teacher's Guide to Type: A New Perspective on Individual Differences in the Classroom.*[5] Read the information carefully and you will soon see *your* child's personality emerging from particular categories. Then you can use the learning-style information to help your child tackle his school assignments from the direction that is most comfortable for him. You might also mention your child's psychological type and learning style to his teacher. There are many educators who will use this information wisely and productively.

An Extraverted Student:

- likes variety and action
- enjoys talking out loud about ideas
- demonstrates energy and enthusiasm
- is stimulated by, and responsive to, people and actions in the environment
- may be easily distracted
- expresses thoughts and feelings openly
- is energized by being with others
- acts before thinking
- is friendly and talkative
- may be impatient with long, slow projects
- values friends and relationships

Learning Styles and Activities for Extraverted Students

1. Allow them to talk about a story or to problem-solve with you before sending them off to work alone.
2. Give them the chance to reconsider their answers since Extraverts may impulsively respond with the first thing that comes to mind.
3. Allow opportunities for trial-and-error learning when using such tools as computers and microscopes, or with math problems, or during spelling exercises. These students generally learn better when the concept follows an actual experience.
4. When concentration is required, these children generally work better if there are no distractions.

An Introverted Student:

- enjoys individual or one-on-one activities
- is energized by ideas
- thinks before acting
- likes to concentrate on a few select tasks at a time
- carefully considers an idea before discussing or making a decision about it
- usually waits for others to make the first move

- may not communicate thoughts and feelings
- needs privacy
- can make him- or herself inconspicuous
- tends to sit back, observe, and reflect
- dislikes interruptions
- must understand an idea or project before attempting it
- pauses before answering and may be uncomfortable with spontaneous questioning
- can ignore distractions

Learning Styles and Activities for Introverted Students

1. After asking a question, pause a few moments before expecting an answer. Introverts like to think before they speak.
2. Introverted students should not be put on the spot by being asked too many questions that require spontaneous answers, or by being asked to be the first to give oral presentations. Tell the teacher that your child needs time to understand new situations fully.
3. Help your introverted child to realize that it is acceptable if he is unable to express enthusiasm immediately. If introverted children compare themselves to the majority of their peers, who are likely to be extraverts, they may question their own tendency to hesitate. Help your child understand that there is nothing wrong with him and that children approach new tasks differently.

A Sensing Student:

- likes precise directions
- enjoys films and other audiovisual presentations
- prefers using skills already learned
- focuses on the present
- works steadily with a realistic idea of how long the task will take
- prefers things that are definite and measurable
- wants material presented step-by-step
- relies on experience rather than theory
- is interested in whatever appeals to the senses
- is likely to recall details well

- may be comfortable with routine exercises that develop skills
- draws on proven methods to solve current problems
- enjoys tradition and custom
- can learn abstract concepts but may become stressed by the task
- wants the facts when discussing an issue and mistrusts vague ideas

Learning Styles and Activities for Sensing Students

1. Straight lectures usually aren't enough to attract the attention of sensing students. Support classroom lessons by using a "hands-on" approach whenever possible. Sensing children usually learn best if they can see something, touch it, and sort it.
2. Provide your child with four or five practical examples each time a new concept is introduced in class. Relate the current task to real people, things, or places in the student's world. For example, have your child search for a chemical in a product found in your home when studying the chemical elements.
3. Sensing students prefer material to be presented in a linear fashion, so they will find outlines an especially helpful study aid.

An Intuitive Student:

- needs opportunities to be creative and original
- likes tasks that require imagination
- enjoys learning new skills more than mastering familiar ones
- dislikes routine
- works in bursts of energy with slow periods in between
- dislikes taking time for precision
- focuses on the future
- may skip over facts or get them wrong
- spends so much time designing an original project that the finished product may not meet expectations
- needs variety

- has a seemingly sporadic approach rather than an ordered, step-by-step approach
- is idealistic

Learning Styles and Activities for Intuitive Students

1. Challenge Intuitive students with problem-solving activities for which there are multiple solutions. (See examples in Chapter 3.)
2. Since Intuitive students tend to grasp new concepts quickly, don't force your child to go over and over practice material.
3. Make an effort to present assignments as a challenge.
4. Hang a calendar in your child's room that clearly specifies deadlines. If the assignments are challenging, Intuitive students will complete them quickly, but they will usually procrastinate with routine assignments.

A Thinking Student:

- values individual achievement over group cooperation
- needs to know *why* things are done
- may enjoy talking with teachers more than with peers
- dislikes small talk
- enjoys library research projects
- enjoys debates
- often finds ideas or things more interesting than people
- needs opportunities to demonstrate competence
- is concerned with truth and justice based on principles
- can be devastated by failure
- prefers information to be presented briefly and concisely
- spontaneously analyzes the flaws in ideas, things, or people
- is task oriented
- needs to know the criteria for grades and evaluations

Learning Styles and Activities for Thinking Students

1. Provide these students with logical outlines of information they are expected to master.
2. Allow them to solve problems by collecting, organizing, and evaluating information.

3. Use brainteasers, puzzles, or games that have "right" answers so they can be challenged and provided with a sense of achievement. (See Chapter 3 for examples.)
4. Tell them what they have done right and explain why it is right.
5. Check their work and provide feedback quickly.

A Feeling Student:

- enjoys sharing information in small groups
- is loyal
- tries to help others feel secure and comfortable
- needs praise
- avoids confrontation and conflict
- is skilled in understanding other people
- is sympathetic
- spontaneously appreciates the good in people and things
- views things from a personal perspective
- is concerned about relationships and harmony
- enjoys pleasing people, even in seemingly unimportant matters
- enjoys subjects that concern people; needs to know how the topic affects people
- has difficulty accepting criticism; sarcasm and ridicule can be devastating

Learning Styles and Activities for Feeling Students

1. Write personal notes of encouragement for the Feeling student, such as "This is wonderful," "Keep up the good work," or "Your ideas are interesting."
2. Make time for some family discussions and group decision-making (especially for Extraverted students).
3. Allow them to practice and drill spelling, vocabulary, or math exercises with other children.
4. Praise their efforts, achievements, and ideas. This type of student does best when praised frequently.

A Judging Student:

- prefers expectations for assignments to be clearly defined
- likes to get things settled and finished
- prefers completing one project before beginning another; too many unfinished projects can cause stress
- doesn't usually appreciate surprises
- needs structure and predictability; frequent changes can be upsetting
- likes to make decisions
- gets assignments in on time
- lives by schedules that are not easily altered
- wants to do things the "right" way and tries to make things happen the way they are "supposed" to
- works best when work can be planned and the plan is followed
- is orderly, organized, and systematic
- generally has good study habits

Learning Styles and Activities for Judging Students

1. These students depend on the consistency and predictability of their daily schedules. Prepare them in advance for any changes in daily procedures. If the day's schedule will be changed in some way, tell them in advance.
2. These students like to budget their time carefully. Having too many unfinished projects can be stressful for them, so allow them to finish some activities before starting new ones.
3. If possible, give Judging children a course outline that shows the topics to be covered on each grading period.

A Perceiving Student:

- is curious
- may begin working on a task before the directions are completed
- acts spontaneously

- likes freedom to move and finds too much desk work to be boring
- is cheerful and brings fun and laughter to the classroom
- enjoys the activity itself more than the result
- enjoys tasks presented as games
- enjoys dramatizations and may like to perform
- copes well with unplanned and unexpected changes and enjoys changes in procedure
- may start too many projects and have difficulty finishing them all
- lets work accumulate and then accomplishes a lot with a last-minute flurry of activity
- may turn in assignments late as a result of poor planning or time management

Learning Styles and Activities for Perceiving Students

1. Help Perceiving children develop plans by helping them determine the latest date at which a project can be started and still meet expectations. Simply instructing them to begin a project as soon as it is assigned works against their natural style.
2. Allow them opportunities to move and be physically active.
3. Allow plenty of time for discussions that do not lead to preconceived conclusions. These students prefer to explore all perspectives on a subject before reaching a conclusion.
4. While expecting behavior to conform to certain standards, allow some flexibility. Too many rules weigh heavily on this type of child, so allow for some fun in each day.

You may have already labeled your child's personality as shy, perfectionist, conformist, rebel, leader, etc. using the above information about psychological type, you can now see why his natural preferences give him these personality characteristics and how they affect his ability to learn. These types are, of course, only generalities about one aspect of your child's complete self. But even a basic understanding of what makes some things easy for him and other things more difficult will make it easier for you to support and to guide his efforts to reach his full potential in school.

In the opening of this chapter you met several children

who, although very different in personality, were all expected to act, respond, and learn in the same manner. This kind of potentially volatile situation can be defused if it is recognized by the parents.

- Greg, the perfectionist, is a Thinking Student. If his parents are aware that he can be devastated by failure, they can provide at-home opportunities for him to demonstrate his competence, as well as to experience small doses of failure.
- Jennifer is inattentive in class because she is an Intuitive Student. Her habit of daydreaming can be used to enhance her studies if her parents encourage the teacher to provide creative opportunities that allow Jennifer to use her imagination.
- Alex needs to be organized because he is a Judging-type. Alex will work well with a teacher who is also highly organized, but if the teacher should be a Perceiving personality who runs the classroom in a haphazard and spontaneous manner, Alex will become quite frustrated and angry.

While each child has a personality type, so does each teacher. Sometimes the two complement each other. But sometimes the personalities clash. Alex and his Perceiving-type teacher, for example, will certainly lock horns on many occasions. And if daydreaming Jennifer has a Sensing-type teacher who insists on a daily routine of practical, realistic, and concrete lessons, neither one will enjoy the positive qualities of the other. Even perfectionist Greg will have trouble with a Feeling-type teacher who takes his requests for curriculum outlines and more detailed information as a personal insult to his or her teaching style.

If your child and his teacher have a personality conflict, information on personality type will help you understand why the problem exists. You can create a learning environment at home that complements your child's personality, but you should also encourage him to accept the fact that some people act and feel differently than he does. Eventually he must learn how to cope with this fact. The information in Chapter 8 will help you work with your child's teacher to make the best of difficult situations.

Just as each child looks different than every other child

physically, so is his ability to take in, process, and use information. If you can zero in on how well (IQ), why (personality type), and in what manner (learning style) your child does this, you can help him work with his strengths and compensate for his weaknesses. When this happens, students feel happy and competent and all other aspects of school success and achievement more readily fall into place.

Resource List

Write

- Center for Applications of Psychological Type
  2720 N.W. 6th Street
  Gainesville, Florida 32609
  This organization is devoted to promoting the ethical and sound use of psychological type.

Books

- *Please Understand Me*
  K. Deirsey and M. Bates
  Prometheus Nemesis Books, 1978
- *A Parent's Guide to Type*
  Charles and Connie Meisgeier
  Consulting Psychologists Press, 1989
- *Frames of Mind: The Theory of Multiple Intelligences*
  Howard Gardner
  Basic Books, 1983

3

"Can't you figure this out for yourself?"

Teaching Your Child How to Think

Nine-year-old Jimmy likes school. He does his homework, studies for tests, and earns good grades. But his mom is worried because it seems that Jimmy has no idea how to think for himself. "He doesn't seem to be able to take a question or problem," she says, "mull it over, and come up with an answer or solution." She has noticed, for example, that if he has not studied a particular fact, he leaves the test question blank without even venturing an educated guess. A particular question on a recent test read: "What product can be made out of cola nuts?" "I can't remember!" Jimmy insisted.

At home, Jimmy asks what his parents feel are endless, unnecessary questions. He often nags them with queries such as: "Why are you washing the fruit?" "Why do construction workers wear hardhats?" "Why do I have to brush my teeth?" "Max won't play with me; what should I do?" Jimmy seems genuinely stymied by everyday problems and runs to his parents for solutions. Many times his parents feel that Jimmy should be able to figure things out for himself.

Obviously, Jimmy's school intelligence is not serving him well in his day-to-day life. His parents have correctly observed that although Jimmy gets good grades in school, he's not very smart.

Smartness

Smartness is not the same thing as intelligence. While intelligence is marked by the ability to grasp facts, smartness is characterized by the ability to go beyond the facts and use such higher-level thinking skills as:

- observation
- classification
- comparison
- contrast
- inference
- imagination
- creativity
- cause and effect
- problem solving

Smartness is a way of thinking about things. Smartness is NOT:

- an unchanging personality trait
- a measure of how *much* a child knows
- fostered by stuffing the mind with information.

Smartness IS:

- a learned skill
- measure of *how* a child learns things
- fostered by challenges that require a child to produce and evaluate ideas.

Will your child grow up to be "smart"? That depends on what he does with the brain he was born with. At birth the brain contains 10 to 15 billion neurons (the cells of the nervous system and the brain). The number of these neurons present at birth is fixed; we can never add on new ones. This is true despite the fact that thousands may die off each day due to natural attrition, the use of drugs or alcohol, illness, or injury. (But since we only use 5 to 10 percent of our neurons, this loss is not cause for great concern.) The fact that we can't maintain or increase the number of our brain cells does not mean that we can't improve our ability to think however. "Smartness" is determined by the number and quality of the connections *between* these cells. But at birth the connections are only potential; they are not actually built until they carry a message from one cell to another. This happens every time your child interacts with his environment; a chemical and electronic response is triggered in his brain, producing and strengthening the connections.[1] How thrilling it is to know that you have the opportunity to increase your child's brainpower simply by offering him a wide variety of stimulating experiences. How frightening it is to consider that the chance to make neurons flourish can be lost through neglect or by misguided attempts to cram the brain full of facts without giving equal time to reflection, imagining, considering, and wondering—the things that quality neuron connections are made of.

The Thinking Process

There are a wealth of scientific studies that document the developmental process of thinking skills. Although they are far too complex to explain in detail in this book, there are some general and basic aspects of how children learn to think that you should know to better help your child make optimal use of his brain. It is known, for example, that 1) thinking develops in stages, 2) the development of thinking skills doesn't happen by accident or osmosis, 3) children can be taught *how* to think.

Stages of Thinking

Thinking skills develop in different stages based on factors such as a child's age and experiences. In 1926, Swiss developmental psychologist Jean Piaget (and many others since then) found that children at given ages show common ways of thinking about things based on their biological mat-

uration and experience with the environment. This development of thinking skills is not an obscure mental process that
can be observed only by trained professionals. You, yourself, can easily see evidence of stages of thinking. For example:

- Almost all 1-year-olds perceive their world based only on
  what their five senses tell them. Therefore, they can see no
  distinction between the past, the present, and the future.
- Most 5-year-olds operate on a concrete, literal level, and so
  they believe what they see. They see that the sun is much
  smaller than a house, and use it as a basis for their convic-
  tions about relative size.
- Most 8-year-olds gain a sense of social justice that brings
  them to realize, for example, that the end does not always
  justify the means.
- The 13-year-old is ready to consider "what if" situations,
  think abstractly, and find logical, alternative solutions to
  everyday problems.

Normal children pass through these stages slowly but surely.
With or without adult guidance, children will pass through
them as they grow and mature. However, the degree to
which the thinking abilities develop depends on how often
their parents and teachers give them opportunities to practice "thinking." The development of thinking skills is sometimes compared to the development of typing skills. A person
who learns to type without instruction or guidance will usually settle for the two-finger method. As he practices typing
with just two fingers, he may acquire a fair degree of capa-
bility, but the skill will never develop much beyond this
basic hunt-and-peck approach. Another person who takes
the time to practice and learn more advanced touch-typing
skills will soon have far greater skill at using the typewriter
with efficiency than the two-finger operator. So too with
thinking skills—give your child the time he needs to practice
and learn higher-level thinking skills so he will be able to
more efficiently use his brain.

Your Role

Your role in helping your child develop thinking skills is to create a home environment that supports not only his academic work, but also encourages intellectual curiosity, the excitement of discovery, and the joy of "figuring it out for yourself."

There are innumerable things you can do to encourage your child's development of higher level thinking skills. You may already do many of these instinctively. But before you jump head first into the activities suggested in this chapter, take a minute to look where you're going. The following list of "Don'ts" will head off problem areas before they can escalate and defeat your efforts.

When Teaching Your Child How to Think:

- DON'T move too fast or attempt too much. Thinking skills develop slowly, *accompanying* physical maturation.
- DON'T expect too much. You will not see immediate results. Developing thinking skills may not even improve classwork or standardized test scores right away—instead, it strives to bring your child beyond the factual, literal level sometimes emphasized in school.
- DON'T barrage your child with facts. Memorizing facts is a low-level thinking skill. A 5-year-old can memorize the fact that the sun is larger than his house, but without an understanding of the concept of distance and size, he hasn't learned anything of value to him.
- DON'T put too much emphasis on right or wrong answers when practicing thinking skills. When the 5-year-old says his house is bigger than the sun because it looks bigger, he's not wrong; on his level of thinking, he's absolutely right. Your job is to guide him to experiences in which he can find out for himself that distance makes objects smaller.

- DON'T solve all your child's problems for him. If you're in the habit of saying, "Here, let me do that for you," you're robbing your child of valuable learning opportunities. Get in the habit of giving your child time to figure things out, think about possibilities, struggle through to a solution. If he asks for your help, give him guidance and suggestions, not solutions.
- DON'T put off trips to museums, theater, and dance performances until your child is "old enough to remember and/or appreciate it." All experiences are "remembered" in some deep region of the mind, and they enrich life in countless, unforeseeable ways. When you have opportunities to expose your child to something new—do it.
- DON'T look for perfection in all work. When your child writes a story just for fun, don't correct the spelling. When your child tells you an exciting story, don't correct his grammar. Give your child a sense of freedom to explore and to take risks.
- DON'T assume your child is learning thinking skills in school. While many educators teach children in ways that promote advanced thinking skills, there are others who seldom rise above questions of factual recall. This happens, in part, due to the available teaching materials. One study found, for example, that of more than 61,000 questions found in the teacher guides, student workbooks, and tests for nine history textbooks, more than 95 percent were devoted to factual recall.[2] (The difference between a factual and a thought-provoking question is the difference between asking, "When was the printing press invented?" and asking, "How has the invention of the printing press improved the quality of your life?")

You can get a quick insight into a teacher's philosophy on teaching thinking skills by examining several of his or her classroom tests. How many of the questions ask for simple recall of facts? How many ask thinking questions like "Why?" "What do you think?" "Compare." "What would happen if . . . ?" This won't tell you everything about a teacher's methods; more may be going on in the classroom than is reflected on tests. But it will tell you where the emphasis lies.

Now that you know what NOT to do, it's time to take a look at specific kinds of thinking skills. The next section will describe the skills of observation, comparison and classification, inference, cause and effect, creativity, and problem solving. It will also tell you how to foster these skills in your child's thinking patterns.

Observation

We all learn through our five senses. What we touch, taste, smell, hear, and see each day become part of us. Our senses are at the core of our ability to relate one experience to another, and they provide the basic information we need to begin the thinking process. Unfortunately, powers of observation grow weak through neglect. We tend not to take in as much information from our environment as we are capable of doing. To prove this point, ask the following questions of yourself and your child:

- What color eyes does your neighbor have?
- Does the door at your school swing in or out?
- Does the clock in your kitchen have a second hand?
- Whose face is on a dime?
- Where is the fire hydrant nearest to your home?

If you are able to answer these questions, your ability to see *and* observe is sharp and you should share this gift and develop it in your child with the following suggestions. If you are unable to answer these questions, you can appreciate how easy it is to look at something and not really see it. Both you and your child will benefit from the exercises on pages 57–60, which will improve the powers of observation.

Comparison and Classification

Comparing and classifying are advanced forms of observing. Your child needs to look at the details of things to see in what ways they are similar or different from other things he knows. This information enables him to put objects and ideas in a certain order based on their characteristics, making it easier to analyze and understand them. Items can be grouped by comparing color, or shape, or size, or function, or in any other variety of categories that children may create, such as "foods I like" or "animals that scare me."

The skills of classification and comparison are closely tied to the development of learning skills. Anything with fur and four legs may be called "dog" by a very young child—until he learns the words he needs to classify cows, cats, and horses. In the same way, to categorize carrots, beans, and corn as "vegetables," a child needs first to have this word in his vocabulary. Therefore, you can develop the skills of classification and comparison by practicing grouping as well as language skills. The games and exercises on pages 61–63 will help you build on these skills.

Inference

Inference is the ability to come to a conclusion based on the facts that are available. It includes hypothesizing and predicting. If your child walked into the bedroom that he had cleaned earlier in the day and found his things thrown all over the room, he might *infer* that his baby sister had been in his room. Or, if your child wakes up in the morning and sees puddles outside he might infer that it had rained during the night. If your child sees a car speeding down the street, he might infer that the driver is in a hurry. He wouldn't know any of these things for certain, but has come to logical conclusions based on what he observes.

At a very early age children learn to take in observable facts and create a plausible explanation. This ability to infer is a part of all problem-solving and data analysis for scientific experiments.

The exercises on pages 64–66 will improve your child's ability to think, infer, and predict. Some will also point out the danger of jumping to a conclusion too quickly or without weighing all the factors. (You may find that you too sometimes "jump to conclusions.")

Cause and Effect

Children experience cause and effect when they realize that one action results in a reaction. At a very early age, children learn, "If I do this, then that will happen." Infants may first see this relationship when their hand accidentally hits their bath water and causes a splash. They will repeat that action over and over again to see the reaction they are capable of causing. The concept of cause and effect is understood by the time children reach school age, but they need practice opportunities to see how cause and effect affects the world in which they live.

This higher-level thinking skill is a key element in the decision-making process. Good decisions are based on the ability to see the effect of one's actions. The activities on pages 66–68 will help your child exercise this skill.

Creativity

Creativity is characterized by an inventive, flexible, and free style of thinking. This enables a person to see new ways to do old things. Some people say, "either you are creative or you aren't." But research and scientific studies say differently. It is strongly believed that habits of thinking that draw out creative abilities can be taught and encouraged.

A creative person shows a flexibility of thought that allows him to see many sides of an issue, several approaches to a problem, and a variety of possible solutions. These thinking tools are a valuable asset for three reasons:

1. Research at the University of New York at Buffalo has shown that students who complete a course in creativity tend to increase their leadership ability, persistence, and initiative as well.
2. English writer and philosopher Samuel Johnson said, "Curiosity is one of the most permanent and certain characteristics of a vigorous mind."
3. Robert W. Olson, author of *The Art of Creative Thinking*, has stated:

- Creative people are able to engage their unconscious minds to solve problems.
- They are more receptive to their own new ideas and to those of others.
- They combine judgment and facts based on their knowledge and experience to select the best solutions.
- They have the energy and commitment to transform their ideas into viable results.[3]

Despite the value of creative thinking abilities, they are often treated as "unimportant" and even discouraged in our children. Research finds a sharp decline in creative powers between the ages of 4 and 10. Four-year-olds are more uninhibited in their zest to explore, seek reasons, take apart, sing, dance, laugh, pretend, and play. But by the time these same children turn 10, this zeal will likely bend to a desire to conform; and they will tackle new projects with caution and doubt highlighted by the question, "How do you want me to do this?"

This decline in creative thinking is not inevitable for children whose parents believe that creative play is not a frivolous activity that should be reserved for infrequent moments of "fun." Think of creativity as a tool that can improve the quality of life. It is a way of overcoming and outsmarting problems in work, play, and life. You can keep it alive by following the guidelines below and by practicing the activities that follow.

Show Through Your Attitude That You Value Creative Thought.

Do you throw away art projects but carefully file report cards? Let your child know that you admire both his academic and creative efforts. Give him opportunities to be a unique and creative member of the family. Think before you react negatively to projects that might make a mess, or ideas that don't exactly mirror your own, or tastes in clothing or music that aren't your choice. If you squash actions or thoughts just because they're not what you would do, you're sending your child a message that says, "Don't think for yourself; just do what I do and say what I say." This mode of thinking won't serve your child well once he steps away from your side.

Allow Your Child Quiet, Reflective Time.

While it is important to provide stimulating experiences for your child, it's also important to give him time for daydreaming, thinking, imagining, and just plain staring at the ceiling. Take a look at your child's day. He's over-scheduled if there's no time in it to do "nothing."

Avoid Dictating What to Do.

When your child comes to you with a problem, try not to give him your solution. Instead, say to him, "What do you think you should do?" Give your child some freedom of thought, and he'll soon learn that he can usually control his environment rather than being controlled by it.

Allow a Certain Amount of Risk-taking.

Your child won't feel comfortable being creative if he has to worry about making a mistake or being "wrong." Let him explore his world, try it on, discard ideas that don't fit, and look for better ones. If he draws a multi-color elephant, don't criticize it; enjoy it. If he wants to erect a backyard tent out of an old blanket, let him try it alone even though you know a better and a faster way to do it. When he walks toward the brook, don't point out all the dangers; stand close by to guard him from harm, but give him room to touch, explore, and discover. The games and exercises on pages 68–71 will help you foster your child's creativity.

Problem Solving

Everyone has problems. How we solve these problems depends on how well we have incorporated the higher-level thinking skills into our daily routines. Many people solve problems by jumping at the first solution that comes to mind; unfortunately, this is not usually the best one. Children can learn to produce superior solutions by taking more time to use their ability to observe, classify, compare, infer, consider cause and effect, and be creative.

The problem-solving process does not come naturally to children; they need guidance, support, and opportunity. For example, when your child is faced with a problem like, "I don't know what to get Jimmy for his birthday," don't give him a solution—help him to observe what Jimmy likes, compare what he has to what he needs, infer from conversations what he wants, and consider what would happen if a particular gift were selected then, based on this information, help your child think of something unique and special.

The following four steps are generally used in creative problem solving:

1. Identify the problem. This step seems so obvious that it is sometimes overlooked. Take time to help your child look closely at what is really wrong. If your child comes home angry at his teacher for being so "picky," it may come out in conversation that the anger really results from the fact that your child failed a test.
2. Brainstorm for possible solutions. Brainstorming is a strategy commonly used for solving problems. It follows a simple process of idea sharing. A problem (as defined in step 1) is presented and everyone in the room takes turns offering possible solutions following these basic rules:

• Any idea is acceptable, no matter how silly or wild.
• No criticism or discussion of ideas is allowed during brainstorming.
• Quantity of ideas is most important; quality will creep in along the way.

3. Choose a solution that might work. Look over the list of suggestions formulated by brainstorming. Encourage your child to choose one that he believes will best solve his problem.
4. Try it out! Take that solution and use it. Make sure your child knows that there is no one "right" or "wrong" answer. If the chosen solution doesn't work out, he should never be too embarrassed or stubborn to go back to step 3 and select another possible solution.

Use this process with problems that come up in your family. Your child will grow to consider this creative problem-solving technique a natural approach to life's dilemmas. The exercises on pages 72–73 will help you foster the skill of creative problem solving.

Exercising the Brain

The following brain teasers, puzzles, riddles, and games stretch the mind to look at things from different perspectives. Some teach children to work around mental roadblocks that cause a type of tunnel vision, others encourage them to concentrate or think logically. Like the muscles of the body, the mind stays in shape with exercise. The more often you can play these games with your child, the more capable of higher-level thinking his mind (and yours!) will become.

As you play, remember: The point is not just to find right or wrong answers, or to find answers quickly. It is to foster opportunities to think in new and interesting ways.

Observation Games and Exercises

1. Gather together a group of household items such as a rubber band, hairbrush, can of soup, toothpaste, pencil, key, etc. Place them on a tray and let your child look at them for 5 to 10 seconds. Take the tray away and ask your child to list as many of the items as he can remember. Bring the tray back to your child and compare his list to the items.

   VARIATION: Let your child look at the tray for a few seconds; take it away and remove one item. Bring the tray back to your child and ask him to guess what's missing. You can keep doing this until all items are removed from the tray.

   AGES: People of all ages can play this game. You can

tailor it to your child's age and abilities by increasing or decreasing the number of items on the tray and the amount of time allowed for observing.

2. For 10 seconds, observe an object, like the refrigerator, and then draw it from memory. See how many minute details, like the manufacturer's name and symbol, or the appropriate side of the hinges and handle, and the ventilation grid, are included. Each time your child plays this game, encourage him to get more and more out of his 10 seconds of observation time.
   AGES: All children who can draw (regardless of talent) can play this game. Your expectations for realistic duplications should, of course, change with the age of the child. You might further challenge older children by asking them to draw the item upside-down.

3. Take apart discarded household items like a clock, camera, or radio, and put them back together. (Cut off electrical wires so they cannot be plugged in.) The first time your child tries this, the results may be discouraging; encourage him, the second time, to spend more time observing the item's construction *before* he dismantles it. He'll soon learn that close observation makes most jobs easier.
   AGES: Children ages 5 to 8 can observe the structure, take apart, and put back together items with three to ten pieces. Children ages 8 to 12 can tackle more complex and numerous pieces, but try to steer them away from major projects like a TV that will serve only to frustrate their efforts.

4. Recount the steps involved in *doing* something like making a cake, or going fishing, or washing the car. You can ask your child to do this before you're about to actually do the activity; this will help him learn to prepare and organize for tasks. Or you can ask him to do this *after* the activity has been completed to help him expand his sense of awareness about what he's just experienced.
   AGES: All children, no matter what the age, will begin this game by naming the obvious, major steps. When they're finished, go back over the process with them to point out the smaller details that were overlooked (like getting things

out of the refrigerator and letting the butter sit at room temperature when making a cake). Expect more and more details each time you play the game.

5. Make a map that charts the route to school, or to the store, or to a friend's house. Include each block, stop sign, red light, store locations, and other landmarks along the way. The next time you make the trip, have your child bring his map and observe closely; let him add omitted details to the map each time you travel that way. It seems that there's always more to add, the more often you look. AGES: For children ages 5 to 8, select a short, familiar route. For children 9 to 12, make the routes longer and expect more details.

6. Look through children's magazines and books for puzzles and games that ask the reader, "In what way are these pictures different?" Or, "How many animals can you find hiding in this picture?" AGES: These games are most often created for children 2 through 8 years old. Only occasionally will you find these kinds of visual puzzles for older children and teens.

7. Call your child's attention to things that he might overlook. When you walk through the park, show him where the wild flowers grow. Point out birds' nests. Watch how the shadow of a tree moves as the sun moves in the sky. When you look for things to observe, you'll never come up empty-handed. AGES: All ages.

8. Describe a room in your house. After noting the obvious, push for the finer details: "What does the ceiling look like?" "What kind of lampshade is in the room?" "What kind of lock is on the door?" AGES: This game is fun for children of all ages.

When Time Is Tight:

1. Direct your dinner conversations to daily observations like, "What was your teacher wearing today?" "Where is the flag in your classroom?" "Were the shades in your

bedroom up or down when you came home from school today?"

2. Ask specific questions about special outings, such as parties and field trips. Ask, for example, "How many children were there?" "What route did you take to get there?" "What did the party room look like?"

3. When riding home from the grocery store, see how many purchases your child can remember. Ask him to name three items that begin with the letter B, or two items that you've never bought before, or the brand name of the butter. (Younger children usually love this game; older children may think it's dumb.)

4. Keep a list of the following questions[4] and make up some of your own. Throw one out for your child to think about on the run, while he's taking a bath, or eating breakfast. You might even slip one into his lunch bag. These will give him "something to think about" until you see him again. If he doesn't know the answer, or is too young to have experienced the situation, challenge him to find the correct answer.

- Which of the following turns is arranged in clockwise direction?
  a. a record on a phonograph
  b. the numbers on a standard telephone dial
  c. the wheels of a forward-moving car when viewed from the left side
  (Solution: a. a record on a phonograph)

- True or false . . . ?
  a. Buttons on a woman's coat are on the right side.
  b. Knives at a dinner setting are placed on the right side.
  c. A car driver sits on the right side.
  d. The Statue of Liberty holds the torch in her right hand.
  e. In his famous pose, Napoleon has his right hand inside his coat.
  f. The American Eagle faces toward the right side.
  g. On a globe, South Africa lies to the right of South America.
  h. The Indian on a nickel faces toward the right side.
  i. The coin-return on a public telephone is on the right side of the box.
  (Solutions: a. false; b. true; c. false; d. true; e. true; f. false; g. true; h. false; i. false.)

Comparison and Classification Games and Exercises

1. Skim through a dictionary to find about twenty nouns that your child knows. Write each one on a separate index card or square piece of paper. Put all the cards into a big bowl, bag, or pot. Have your child pull out two cards and read aloud the selected nouns. Ask your child to think of ways in which these two items are alike. For example: If your child pulls out the words "baseball" and "chair," he must find characteristics or uses that are common to both. At first your child (and you!) may say, "They're not the same at all!" But that's where *thinking* comes in. Baseballs and chairs are both found in baseball stadiums. They are both used while enjoying recreation. Some chairs are solid to the touch and so are baseballs. Some chairs are white like baseballs. Both can get soiled if you rub dirt on them. Neither one is alive. Both get worn out and are eventually discarded. And so on, and on. . . .
   VARIATION: To exercise language skills while using these cards, tell your child to pull out one noun card and tell you all the characteristics of that word. The word "baseball" for example, might elicit, "solid, smooth, white and red, round, a line of stitching making bumps, it doesn't bounce, it's heavier than a Ping-Pong ball."
   HINT: To get the most out of these games, give your child lots of time, and when he says, "I can't think of any more," always challenge him to find "just one more." Usually, he will.
   AGES: All ages. You must, however, choose nouns that you know are familiar to your child. If your child is unable to read the words he chooses, read them for him. Also, you can make the game a bit easier for young children (ages 5 to 8) by asking for ways in which the nouns they select are "different," or by choosing nouns that you know are similar such as, "car, truck, train, airplane," etc.

2. Most children find collections of anything absolutely fascinating. If your child already collects baseball cards,

or bottle caps, or stamps, or shells, or even adventure figures, use this collection to improve his ability to classify and compare. If your child doesn't have a collection in the works, help him start one.

When your child says, "Look at my rocks!" ask him to tell about them. How are they alike? How are they different? What are their characteristics? See if the collection can be subdivided into large rocks, white rocks, heavy rocks, etc. Encourage your child to organize and display his collection. A bunch of bottle caps in a bag are no more than just that. But when they are taken out, inspected, categorized, labeled, and displayed, they become a thinking activity.

AGES: All ages.

3. This game pushes children to search through the categories already established in their minds to find reasons why a "funny little man" likes certain things, but doesn't like other things. The game can run for hours or even days.

Tell your child that you know a funny little man who likes certain things very much, but who very much dislikes other things. For example, he likes boots, but dislikes shoes. (Can you guess why?) He likes trees, but dislikes leaves. He likes wool, but dislikes yarn. Your child will try to find patterns in these likes and dislikes. Let him keep searching as you keep making up more clues. Don't give in too soon and give him the answer. Let him think for a while.

If you haven't guessed by now, the answer is: The funny little man likes words with double letters and dislikes words without double letters. That's why he likes gra*ss*, but dislikes lawns, and he likes pu*dd*les, but dislikes water.

As your child puts together an idea of a possible solution, he'll ask something like, "Does he like cars?" You can answer with another clue: "No. He doesn't like trains or planes either, but he does like scooters." When your child has solved the puzzle (or when you give away the answer), you can still keep the game going as both of you think of more likes and dislikes.

AGES: This game is appropriate only for children who know how to spell the words you'll be using. You can play a variation of this game with younger children by creating categories of likes and dislikes that are more readily understood. You might say, for example, that the funny little man likes coats but dislikes bathing suits; he likes boots but dislikes sandals, etc., to convey the idea that he likes things that keep him warm.

When Time Is Tight:

1. In daily conversations ask your child questions that will lead him to note similarities and differences in the world around him. Ask, for example, "In what ways is your teacher this year different from the one you had last year?" When you begin to ask questions of comparison you may get short answers like "Nothin' " or "I don't know." Until your child grows more used to observing and comparing, you might have to make your questions more specific. "Does this teacher give more or less homework than your teacher last year?"

2. Ask your child to help you when you have a job to do that requires sorting (another word for classifying). This includes matching socks, putting away food, sorting nails, screws, etc.

3. When it's time to clean up your child's bedroom or playroom, engage his help. Let him find and organize items that are alike. Tell him to put action figures in this box, building blocks in that box, and doll accessories in the bottom drawer. It's probably easier and faster if you do it yourself, but it's also a learning opportunity for your child when time for home lessons is hard to come by.

4. Look for things to compare when you're running errands. Point out how your car is different from and yet the same as the car in front of you. When shopping, compare prices of similar items. When walking through the park, compare the shapes of various leaves. Use the world around you— wherever you are and whatever you're doing—to teach your child to observe, compare, and classify.

Inference Games and Exercises

1. Show your young child pictures of people in magazines or books. Ask him to guess (infer) how the person feels. Ask him to explain why he thinks they feel that way.
   AGES: 5 to 8.

2. When reading to your young child, stop occasionally to ask "why" questions. "Why do you think the monkey feels unhappy?" "Why did the boy leave his dog at home?" "Why is the girl crying?"
   AGES: 5 to 8.

3. Discuss TV weather reports. Ask your child to observe how tomorrow's weather is predicted. Talk about why these weather reports are sometimes wrong.
   AGES: All ages.

4. Gather together a group of household items that you can make noises with (rubber bands, pencil sharpeners, beans in a can, wooden spoons, etc.). Arrange your seating so that your child can't see you; have him sit facing away from you or just around the corner. Then make a noise with one of the items and ask him to infer what object you're using.
   AGES: 5 to 8.

5. Ask your child to infer what objects you've used to make impressions in clay. Using several pieces of flattened non-hardening clay, press household objects like a key, phone cord, fork, cabinet handle, door knob, etc., against each one. Ask your child to guess what objects in the room made those marks. Give him fresh clay to make impressions of the objects he suspects you used and then match them to your clay samples. This will teach him how comparisons can confirm or disprove solutions.
   AGES: All ages.

6. Thought games are especially challenging for children 8 to 12 years old. Give them the following clues and then plenty of time to solve the mysteries:

- Detectives found a man lying dead on his kitchen floor. The only clue they had to solve the case was a 5-inch stick and a puddle of a sticky red substance that were found on the floor nearby. How did the man die? (Solution: The man ate a poisoned ice pop.)
- A man lay near death in a hospital room. His wife was riding in the hospital elevator on her way up to see him when the elevator jostled to an abrupt stop and the lights went out. She knew that at that moment that her husband would probably not be alive when she got up to his room. Why did she think that? (Solution: The elevator stopped because of an electrical blackout. This would cause the respirator to shut down and most likely cause her husband's death.)
- A man is captured and placed into a cell that has a dirt floor and cement walls that are 5 feet wide, 20 feet high, and 20 feet deep beneath the ground. The top of the cell, however, does not have a ceiling; he can see the sky above. After a few minutes thought, the man begins to dig down into the dirt floor. What is his escape plan? (Solution: He's going to dig out a pile of dirt that he will then climb up on and escape over the top.)

When Time Is Tight:

1. Use daily conversations to help your child practice making inferences. Encourage him to make predictions and explain "why." When he goes off to play a game of organized sports, ask him to explain why he thinks his team will win or lose. When he says he's going to be bored by something, get him to explain why. Don't accept an "I don't know, I just don't think so" kind of answer. Help him consider the facts that he has already observed that have brought him to make his conclusions.

2. Use the following short jokes to point out to your older child (ages 9 to 12) the danger of jumping to conclusions when looking at given facts:

- Imagine that you are in the house during an electrical blackout. You have on hand an oil lamp, a candle, and a

kerosene heater; but you have only one match. Which should you light first? (Answer: the match).
- A man walks into a bar and immediately says, "Ouch!" What do you think happened? (Answer: He hurt himself by walking into a bar—the metal kind.)
- Two baseball teams played a full 9 innings, and the final score was 5 to 3. But the fans didn't see a single man touch homeplate. How could this happen? (Answer: The players were all girls.).

VARIATION: A young boy and his father are in a car crash. The father dies and the boy is brought to the local hospital for emergency surgery. Once there, the surgeon looks at the boy and says, "I can't operate on this boy. He is my son." How is this possible? (Answer: The surgeon is the boy's mother.)

- You have two coins that total 15 cents, but one isn't a nickel. How is that possible? (Answer: You have a dime and a nickel. One—the dime—is not a nickel.)
- How much dirt is there in a hole 2 feet deep, 2 feet long, and 2 feet wide? (Answer: None; a hole is empty.)
- How many months have 28 days? (Answer: All of them.)
- If a plane crashes on the border of Canada and the United States, where would the survivors be buried? (Answer: Nowhere; you don't bury survivors.)

Cause-and-Effect Games and Exercises

1. Before blowing up balloons for some fun or for a party, put a pinhole in one of them. With your child in the room, or with his help, blow up a few balloons and then try to blow up the one with the hole in it. See if your child can figure out why that one won't blow up.
   AGE: All ages. After a bit of experimenting, some older children will be able to explain the problem to you. If your child doesn't know why the balloon won't blow up, show him the hole and explain how air can seep through such a tiny place.

2. When reading a story to your child, stop occasionally to ask, "What do you think will happen next?" Or, stop just

2. short of the ending and ask your child to decide what will happen at the end.

AGES: Use this activity for as long as you read aloud to your children. Some children enjoy listening to stories well into junior high. If you no longer read aloud to your child, help him find cause-and-effect relationships in the books he is reading. Ask him to tell you what the book is about so far; then encourage him to guess what will happen next.

3. Exercise cause-and-effect thinking skills through "what if" statements:

- What would happen if I didn't water the plants?
- What would happen if we ate only junk food?
- What would happen if it rained for one hundred days?

Everyone playing the game must try to list ten different effects of the given situation. Your child's first response to the first question might be, "The plant would die. That's all; there's nothing else to say." Encourage him to consider what would happen to the leaves, the dirt, the appearance, etc. Remember: higher-level thinking skills need time to develop.

AGES: With children ages 5 to 8, you can make a game of taking turns thinking of "what ifs." With older children you can encourage this kind of thinking by responding to their own statements with "what if" questions. For example:

Child: "I hate when it rains."
Parent: "What do you think would happen if it never rained again?"

When Time Is Tight:

1. Get into the habit of talking out loud as you go about your daily activities. While you're cooking you might point out to your young child, "I want these vegetables to soften and cook, so I'll put them in this pot of water on the stove. When the water gets hot enough and boils, the

vegetables will be ready to eat." Or, before you go out on a cloudy day, say to your child, "I think I'll bring my umbrella even though it's not raining. Those clouds make me think it may rain later."

2. When there's time, remember to explain the "why" of things. Instead of handing your child his jacket with a quick, "Put this on," explain what you're thinking—"I want you to wear this in the morning while it's cool, but when the sun comes out later you probably won't need it." And, when you say to your child, "Get your toys off the stairs," remember to add, "If they're left on the stairs, someone may trip over them and get hurt."

3. In addition to explaining the "why" of the things you say and do, occasionally respond to your children's statements with your own "whys":

Child: "Come on. Hurry up."
Parent: "Why are you in such a hurry?"

Child: "I have nothing to do."
Parent: "Why do you think you always feel bored on Sunday afternoons?"

Child: "I can't wait to go to Missy's house."
Parent: "Why?"
Child: " 'Cause I like it there."
Parent: (pushing the child to be more specific) "What do you do there that's so much fun?"

Creativity Games and Exercises

1. Keep a junk box in your house. Fill it with things like yarn, clay, buttons, fabrics, glue, wood pieces, foam rubber, thread, egg cartons, tape, magnets, plastic containers, wire, jars, fur, etc. When you bring it out for play, don't tell your child exactly what to do and how to do it. Let him create! All you need to give is your attention and support.

AGES: All ages.

VARIATIONS:

- Have your child randomly pull three pieces of junk out of the box. Challenge him to make "something" using all three pieces and anything else he needs that he can find around the house.

AGES: All ages.

- With his eyes closed, have your child take out one piece of junk from the box. Ask him to list in one minute all its possible uses. For example, if your child pulls out a rock, it could be used as a paperweight, a door stop, a garden decoration, or a way to smash open a piggy bank.

2. Don't throw away your old clothing. Throw it in a large box and bring it out for special dress-up occasions, neighborhood plays, and on any rainy day when pretend play is just what your child needs to pass the time creatively.

    AGES: Although all kids love to act out pretend characters, only younger ones will do it for show. Leave the box where older children can find it; and one day they may drop their inhibitions long enough to enjoy the fun of dress-up when no one is looking.

    HINT: Try to avoid pre-set art projects like paint-by-numbers art. Although they sometimes give a child a feeling of accomplishment, they don't allow him to be creative and decide on his own colors, patterns, and designs.

3. Next time you and your child are outdoors on a partly cloudy day, take some time to find cloud pictures. If you look at a cloud enough and with enough imagination, you'll find it looks just like (*something*)!

4. Create and read droodles—simple line drawings with clever titles that are creative and often humorous. Some common droodles are:

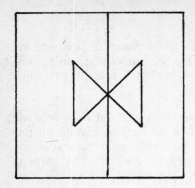

If your child says it's a gift package, say, "Good. What else could it be?" With time and imagination, he might consider a butterfly on a telephone line, or a man with a bow tie stuck between closed elevator doors, or any other of a hundred possibilities.

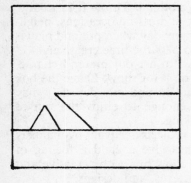

Perhaps: A ship arriving too late to save a drowning witch.

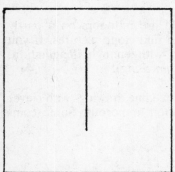

If your child says, "A line on a piece of paper," use the guidelines above to encourage him to become more playful and flexible in his thinking. He should eventually be able at least to see that this could be a picture of what's left when the ice pop is all gone.

HINT: There are no "right" or "wrong" answers to droodles.
AGES: All kids love droodles. Five- to 8-year-olds like to read them; older children often enjoy making their own.

When Time Is Tight:

1. Watch for opportunities to compliment your child on his creativity. If he should do something in a particularly clever or unique way, note and encourage his efforts.
2. Leave a droodle (see number 4 above) on the kitchen table or taped to your child's mirror. Challenge him to invent five titles by dinner time.
3. Make creative tools (see number 1 above) available on those days when you're not around and you suspect your child may have "nothing to do."
4. Do quick puzzles that challenge the way your older child thinks. You might try some of these:

$\dfrac{\text{man}}{\text{board}}$ = man overboard

1,001,000 = one in a million

$\overline{\text{reading}}$ = reading between the lines

$\dfrac{\text{stand}}{\text{i}}$ = I understand

$\dfrac{0}{\substack{\text{M.D.} \\ \text{Ph.D.}}}$ = two degrees below zero

he's/himself = he's beside himself

ecnalg = glance backwards

_____ program = space program

5. Let your younger child use creative playthings even though they may make a mess. (These include things like paint, building blocks, clay, markers, scissors, glue, etc.)
6. Encourage your child to explore the world and to ask "why" and "how" questions.

Problem-Solving Games and Exercises

1. Give your child problem-solving opportunities. The "What if . . ." game described on page 67 for practicing cause-and-effective relationships can also be used to practice problem-solving. Using the process described earlier, sit down with a pad and pencil and brainstorm solutions to problems like:

   • "What if you are invited to two birthday parties on the same day?"
   • "What if you get lost at the shopping mall?"
   • "What if a stranger offers you candy?"
   • "What if your friend breaks your favorite toy?"

   AGES: All ages; just adjust the problems to fit the background experiences of your child.

2. Play "product improvement." This game is used in industry to produce "new and improved" merchandise. For instance, you might put a household product like a coffee cup on the table, then ask your child to brainstorm with you ways to make a better cup. Consider these possibilities: color, shape, form, and texture.
   What can you add? subtract? make stronger or larger? lighter or smaller? Find new ways to use it.
   AGES: All ages. Make the product something your child uses.

3. Put a small object in a shoe-box lid on the table. Ask your child to show you how many ways he can make that object move without touching it. (Possible solutions include moving the box lid, moving the table, banging on the table, using something else like a spoon to move the object, or asking someone else to move the object.)
   AGES: All ages.

4. Place a small object inside an empty paper-towel tube. Put the tube on a table. Tell your child to stand three feet away from the table. Ask him to find ways to get the object out of that tube without crossing the imaginary line

in front of him. (Possible solutions include: Since no one said your child couldn't walk *away* from the table, he can get a broomstick to reach over, slip through the tube and make the object slide out. He might get a baseball bat and attempt to knock the table over. Or, he might simply ask you to please hand him the object in that tube.)
AGES: 9 to 12.

5. Define a space from Point A to Point B. Ask your child to think of as many ways as possible to cross over that area. (Possible solutions: walk; run; skip, hop on two feet; hop on one foot; crawl; slither; do all of these backward; do cartwheels.)
AGES: 5 to 12.

When Time Is Tight:

1. Give your child time and opportunities to solve his own daily problems with your guidance but not your interference.

2. Play "What if . . ." (see number 1, page 67) while you're driving your car, or washing your dishes, or whenever the two of you are together.

3. When something like the TV or the toaster or the car breaks down, take the opportunity to brainstorm ways to invent a similar product that wouldn't have these problems.

4. When your child has a real life problem, *make* time to guide him through the steps of problem-solving.

Thinking Skills in School

For the last twenty years, higher-level thinking skills have taken a back seat in many American classrooms. In the 1970s open education was in style. This method of teaching held that children learn best when they are allowed to develop at their own pace. Unfortunately, when theory met practice, too many educators lost sight of the original intent and thought "open classroom" meant tearing down classroom walls and letting children do whatever they wanted. The results were most often disastrous.

The 1980s saw a backlash against "open" education and a return to more traditional practices. Structured classroom settings, workbooks, ditto sheets, and memorization drills returned with a vengeance. Kindergartners were struggling with homework; first graders were taking standardized tests before they could read properly; 8-year-olds were giving up their recess time to "fit in" computer literacy courses; and 10-year-olds were practicing for state-mandated testing programs.

Two notable drawbacks came out of this "back to basics" approach. Many teachers could not find time to practice higher levels of critical or creative thinking, and the National Assessment for Educational Progress found that although most students had an acceptable grasp of basic facts, they were not able to reason, understand, or apply that knowledge.

Fortunately for your child, the trend in educational methods for the 1990s points to increased attention to teaching children how to think.

- The Association for Supervision and Curriculum Development reports that nine out of ten of its surveyed members favor making better instruction in thinking skills a major priority.
- In 1989 a coalition of no less than twenty-seven of the nation's major education groups, including the National Education Association, drew up a five-part agenda to promote thinking skills in the schools. The primary focus will be on improving the teaching of thinking skills by upgrading teacher preservice and in-service training, working with publishers of textbooks and tests, and escalating research into thinking.

If both teachers and parents use and encourage higher-level thinking skills, this generation of students will certainly become the creative thinkers of tomorrow who will be able to confront our country's ills and find acceptable solutions.

Resource List

Write

- *Invent America.* Sponsored by the U.S. Patent Model Foundation, and by several corporations including K-Mart, MasterCard, Dow Chemical, and Pepsico., this nonprofit program asks youngsters in kindergarten through eighth grade to invent solutions to everyday problems. For a starter packet, send $2.75 (for postage and handling) to Invent America, 510 King Street, Suite 420, Dept. BHG, Alexandria, Virginia 22314.
- The National Invention Contest. The *Weekly Reader*, a children's newspaper, receives hundreds of thousands of entries to its annual competition. Past winners have received $250 savings bonds and a trip to Washington, D.C. Details on the contest are usually announced in one of the newspaper's October issues. For more information, write to *Weekly Reader*, 245 Long Hill Road, Dept. BHG, Middletown, Connecticut 06457.

Books

- *A New Way to Use Your Brain: Developing Thinking Skills in Children*
  Darlene Freeman
  Trillium Press, 1981
- *How to Raise a Brighter Child*
  Joan Beck
  Pocket Books, 1987
- *Plans for Children: Raising a Brighter Child in Ten Minutes a Day*
  Jeanne K. Hanson
  Putnam Publishing Group, 1982
- *Mind Joggers: Five to Fifteen Minute Activities That Make Kids Think*
  Sue Petershene
  The Center for Applied Research in Education, 1985.

Video Cassettes

- *Braingames*, Volumes 1, 2, and 3
  HBO Video (catalog #EMI 3259) VHS and Beta
  This series presents interactive video cassettes that integrate history, art, music, culture, and sports.
- *Einstein*
  Vestron Video (catalog #VES 1091) VHS and Beta
  An outstanding NOVA program, *Einstein* is an insightful film portrait of the man whose ideas changed the way we see, think, and manage our world.

Computer Software

- *Think Quick!*
  The Learning Company (1-800-852-2255)
  Ages: 7 to 14
  Apple II Series, IBM/Tandy and compatibles
  This is an animated adventure game that helps children develop important thinking skills.
- *Rocky's Boots*
  The Learning Company (1-800-852-2255)
  Ages: 9–up
  Apple II Series, IBM/Tandy and compatibles, Commodore 64/128 also available
  This program develops logical thinking and problem-solving skills that are important in math and science.
- *Gertrude's Secrets: Early Thinking Skills*
  The Learning Company (1-800-852-2255)
  Grade levels: Kindergarten to 4th grade.
  Apple, Commodore 64, IBM and compatibles
  This program presents seven easy games that build a child's basic thinking and problem-solving abilities.

4

"Will five bucks make kids work harder?"

Using Rewards and Penalties to Motivate

Ten-year-old Karen didn't seem interested in earning good grades in school. Her parents knew she had the potential to be an A student, if she would only try. One day they offered her what some people would call a bribe. "Every time you get an A on a test," they told her, "we'll give you five dollars." They hoped this would be the motivation Karen needed to improve her grades.

Across the street, 10-year-old Lois was not doing her best in school either. Her parents decided to motivate her by punishing her every time she got an F on a test. For her last failing grade, Lois's dad smacked her hands five times with a ruler and sent her to bed without supper. "That should push her to work harder," he thought.

Will Karen and Lois do better next time? Maybe—but they won't do it because of an inner need to achieve. Volumes of research consistently show that punishment does not build self-discipline or inner motivation. Lois may do better the next time to avoid being hurt by her father, but as soon as that external motivation is taken away, she will slide back into poor work habits again. Lois may even grow not to care if she gets hit, and eventually she will be too old for this kind of punishment. What will her father do then to get her to do her school work?

Karen's parents took the opposite approach of trying to motivate their daughter with a monetary reward. They may find that this will encourage Karen to get more A's in school, but it too has its problems. The "five bucks" approach will not teach Karen to enjoy learning; it will cost her parents a fortune if they find that Karen will work only for money, and when used as the sole means of motivation, it does not teach discipline.

"Well," you're probably asking yourself, "if rewards don't motivate kids to be self-disciplined and punishment doesn't do it either, what does?" There *is* a middle ground that many researchers believe is built on a particular style of parenting. In one specific study, four Stanford University researchers found that differences in parental style have a distinct effect on the school performance of adolescents. They examined three styles of parenting: "authoritarian," "permissive," and "authoritative."

In *authoritarian* households, "parents attempt to shape, control and evaluate the behavior and attitudes of their children with an absolute set of standards; parents emphasize obedience, work, tradition, and the preservation of order; verbal give-and-take between parent and child is discouraged."

In *permissive* households, "parents are tolerant and accepting toward the child's impulses, use as little punishment as possible, make few demands for mature behavior, and allow considerable self-regulation by the child."

Authoritative households contain the following elements: "an expectation of mature behavior from the child and clear setting of standards by the parents; firm enforcement of rules and standards, encouragement of the child's independence and individuality; open communication between parents and children; and the recognition of the rights of both parents and children."

The researchers distributed questionnaires to 7,836 high school students and their parents. Experimenters then used the questionnaires to determine the parenting style prevalent in each family. In general, they found that authoritarian parents were those who punished their children for poor grades and failed to reward them for good ones. Permissive parents didn't care about their children's grades one way or the other and showed no interest in their homework. Authoritative parents were those who praised their children when they got good grades, and rewarded them by giving them more freedom to make decisions. They responded to poor grades by taking away freedom, encouraging greater effort, and offering to help with homework.

The researchers found that both the authoritarian and the permissive styles were associated with relatively poor grades. The authoritative parenting style, however, was associated with relatively good grades.[1]

The rest of this chapter will help you assume an authoritative parenting style that will encourage your child to do well in school by helping him to become *self*-disciplined. This characteristic is best nurtured through the consistent use of social and concrete rewards, realistic goal-setting, positive expectations, interest-tapping, and the occasional use of penalties.

Social Rewards

Social rewards don't cost anything, their supply is limitless, and most children will literally stand on their heads to get them. They are positive consequences that motivate through the use of praise, recognition, approval, and attention. This "pat-on-the-back" type of motivation is what makes you *want* to do your best work for the boss who consistently acknowledges your efforts with words of praise and gratitude. It is also what makes you feel defiant, resentful, and prone to produce sloppy work for the boss who harps on small mistakes and ignores your achievements. As you look for ways to motivate your child to do well in school, begin by developing a consistent system of social rewards. Give your child the same kind of positive attention that all working people crave.

In the beginning you may need to look closely at your child's school work to find things worthy of praise. Pay attention and "catch" your child doing *something* good. If he finishes two homework problems before he begins to whine, ignore the complaining and comment on the completed work: "You've made a good start; these two problems are done well." When your child brings home a test, don't immediately bring attention to the errors; first comment on the ones that are correct: "It looks like your studying paid off; you answered these questions correctly. Now let's see if together we can correct these errors."

These kinds of supportive comments have been found to influence children's internal motivation. A 1987 study compared children who worked alone, without an adult to give verbal feedback, to children who were encouraged by an adult with words like:

"That was a good guess."

"You're really doing pretty good."

"You have some good ideas."

The study found that the children who received verbal support while they worked persisted longer, raised their performance level, were more willing to undertake difficult tasks, and had a higher degree of success.[2] What wonderful results from such a simple strategy!

As you attempt to motivate your child with words of praise, make an effort to be specific. Avoid using vague statements such as, "That's wonderful," or, "You're doing a good job." They don't tell a child exactly what it is you like. Children will believe a compliment, store it for future reference, and repeat the admired behavior when it focuses on a specific action. The following examples will show how vague statements can be turned into specific ones.

Vague: "I was so happy when your teacher told me you did well in school today."

Specific: "I was so happy when your teacher told me that you came to class prepared with all of last night's homework and that you paid attention during class."

Vague: "I like the way you've changed your attitude toward school work."

Specific: "I like the way you've been doing your homework without complaining and have been studying to improve your grades."

Vague: "This second composition looks better than the first one."

Specific: "This second composition looks better than the

first one because you've fixed the spelling errors and you've improved your handwriting."

These kinds of specific statements will also make it easier to follow the rule of giving social rewards that says, "Praise the act, not the whole child." When you focus your attention on observable actions ("You followed the directions perfectly"), you avoid labeling the child ("You're a good boy"). This is very important because children often see an implication in this label that says, "If I'm good when I do things right, I must be bad when I do them wrong." And this is not true. A child's actions are good or bad—never the whole child himself. A child is a human being who needs to know that he is worthy of your love no matter what he does.

Another rule says, "When you give your child praise, positive attention and approval, do it without conditions." Don't send mixed messages like:

"You wrote all your letters so well; it's about time."

"Your teacher said you're paying attention in class now. Why couldn't you do that before?"

"Well, it's about time you got it right."

All children want their parents' attention. If they can't get positive attention, they'll misbehave in ways that they know will get their negative attention, because anything is better than nothing. Teach your child that honest effort and achievement are valued by you and, therefore, are all that's needed to gain your attention, approval, and recognition.

Concrete Rewards

Social rewards alone often encourage children to do well in school. Some children, however, may initially need concrete rewards to get them working on academic tasks that are difficult for them. Concrete rewards are tangible items or privileges such as food, toys, a trip to the movies, or extra TV-watching time. These kinds of rewards are most effectively used to enforce what is sometimes called "Grandma's Rule," which says that the reward is dependent on good behavior. You might say to your child for example, "You can have a snack when you work on your homework for twenty minutes." Or, "If your teacher tells me that you've done your best to prepare for Friday's history test—that means paying attention in class, doing your homework, and taking notes when you should—then we'll go to the movies together on Friday night." These kinds of rewards can help children develop a positive attitude toward learning.

Like social rewards, concrete rewards should be given for very specific actions, rather than for vague generalities. This lets your child know exactly what is expected of him and what he's being rewarded for, which in turn encourages him to repeat these specific actions. The following examples illustrate the difference between vague and specific behaviors.

Vague: "You can watch extra TV tonight if you do what you know you should in school."

Specific: "You can watch an extra half hour of TV tonight if your teacher tells me that you paid attention in class and completed all your classwork on time." (You can only reward in-class activities if you know you'll be able to talk to the teacher at the end of the school day.)

Vague: "You can have a treat when you finish your homework."

Specific: "You can have a piece of cake when you finish your ten math problems, read your history assignment, and answer the five questions at the end of the chapter."

Concrete rewards should be given as quickly as possible after the desired act is completed. If, for example, you promise a chocolate cake for doing homework, make sure you have a chocolate cake in the house. If you have to say when the homework is finished, "When I go shopping on Saturday, I'll buy you a chocolate cake," the motivating effect of the reward will be completely lost by the time Saturday comes around.

Money

Giving a child money for his good grades and/or acceptable school performance is another example of using concrete rewards to motivate. But because using money as a reward elicits strong opinions about bribery and mercenary tactics it needs to be addressed separately from food, toys, and privileges. The question of monetary rewards has recently grown past, "Should parents give bucks for good grades?" to "Should school systems use money to make students perform?" Now, not only are parents wondering if money can make their children do better in school, school systems are experimenting with the possibility. An article in *Children* magazine has reported that:

- Tennyson High School in Hayward, California, will pay $250 each to seventy-five "at-risk" ninth-graders this year if they pass courses and keep absences to no more than ten per semester.
- In the Red Bank Regional High School in Little Silver, New Jersey, seventy-seven at-risk students receive a bi-weekly check for $50 from the district for showing up at school regularly and on time, completing homework and behaving in class.
- In Cleveland, Ohio, public school students can earn up to $5,400—which must be used for post-secondary education—during their six years of junior high and high school. For each A a student receives, the district puts $40 in an escrow account; for each B, $20; and for each C, $10. A $10 bonus is added for any major project or honors course a student tackles.

At this point, these programs appear to be successful, but they are not without critics. Many educators and child development experts believe that paying students to do well will not instill a long-term commitment to learning, nor will it help them develop internal controls that they'll need to succeed outside of the school environment.[3]

It is our belief that an occasional monetary reward for work particularly well done or for the completion of a difficult task will fit easily into a family's program of positive reinforcement. This is especially true when the promise of money motivates a child to work for something special, like the pair of $50 sneakers that all of his friends are wearing. However, when money is used without backup social rewards and/or for an extended period of time, it is not a good idea. Under these conditions, monetary rewards will reduce your chances of convincing your child that knowledge is a wonderful thing that should be sought after for its own sake.

Token Rewards

Your child may be motivated to do his school work by the promise of an activity that you cannot give right away. These kinds of activities include things like a movie, or a fishing trip, or a sleep-over party. When you want to use these kinds of rewards, be sure to also give him a token reward each day. Token rewards are visible signs of accomplishment such as stickers or stars on a progress chart that can be collected and traded in for a promised concrete reward. These help children keep count of their successes, and they keep the connection between actions and the promised long-term reward alive.

For example, 6-year-old Heather had a list of sight words to read out loud every night. Every night she dragged this simple 10-minute assignment into a 30-minute battle. She would procrastinate, whine, cry, and eventually holler, "I hate doing this. I won't do it!"

When she wasn't complaining about her homework, Heather pestered her parents to allow her friend Jody to sleep overnight. Finally one Monday night, after struggling with the sight-word problem for half an hour, her parents decided to make a deal. "If you read your sight words aloud without any noise or complaining on Tuesday, Wednesday, and Thursday nights, Jody can sleep over on Friday night. Thursday night, Heather's progress chart looked like this:

Behavior	Tuesday	Wednesday	Thursday
homework	*	*	*
without noise			

Heather earned her sleep-over, her parents gained an extra 20 minutes of peace each night, and Heather found out that the assignment was not as difficult and awful as she thought. Next week, Heather's parents will offer a smaller reward and will stretch out the time period for collection. This will continue each week until Heather's school work becomes routine and she no longer needs concrete rewards.

Phasing-out Concrete Rewards

Phasing-out concrete rewards is an important part of teaching children self-discipline. In the beginning, these rewards should be given every time the desired behavior is put into action (or an honest attempt to do so is made). Every little step in the right direction should be recognized. Then, once the behavior is established as a routine part of schooling, you should give rewards less and less frequently until you phase them out completely. When you see that your child has replaced his bad habits and/or negative attitudes with more positive ones, there's no longer a need to reward him with material things or privileges.

Two Tips for Using Concrete Rewards

1. Don't give the reward unless it is earned.
   Once you decide to use concrete rewards to try to motivate your child, you must promise yourself that you will *not* give the rewards unless your child performs the desired act. Let's say, for example, that you tell your child that he can have a pizza party with two of his friends if he studies at least 15 minutes *every* night that week for his history test on Friday. On Thursday night his progress chart shows that he did not study on Tuesday and Wednesday nights. If you want the reward system to work in the

future, then you must cancel the pizza party. There's no need to nag or yell at your child for not achieving the goal. Give him words of encouragement for next time and then stand firm on the terms of the deal: No study = no pizza party.

2. Use concrete rewards along with social rewards.

When you combine your child's desire to earn concrete rewards with your positive attention and approval, you create a very strong core of motivation. "I'm so happy to see that you've picked out a challenging book for your book report. Come in the kitchen and tell me about it and I'll make you a big bowl of popcorn." Later you can prompt self-praise by commenting, "You must feel real good about the high score you got on this test." As you gradually phase out the concrete and social rewards, your child will be getting into the habit of doing his best just because it makes *him* feel good about himself.

Other Positive Motivators

Rewards are not the only things you can use to motivate your child to do well in school. At the same time that you give praise, approval, and occasional material rewards, try the following other positive motivators.

Help Your Child Set Goals

A goal is something that children want to accomplish or get done. Setting a goal each day or each week can give your child something specific to work toward; achieving the stated goal will then give him a sense of competency and self-esteem. This process of setting, striving, and achieving will help your child want to achieve more.

Unfortunately, you cannot set the goals for your child. If you say, "I want you to start reading the book for your book report three weeks before the report is due," you are not setting a goal, but giving him an order. But you may be able to lead your child to set his own goal if you remind him about the problems that have come up in the past when book-report reading was put off until the last minute. Once he says he wants to plan ahead this time, have him put that goal in writing and hang it where he can easily see it.

> "I will start reading the book for my book report three weeks before it's due."

When your child does begin reading three weeks in advance of the due date, be sure to recognize the effort with praise and attention. Each time your child successfully meets a goal he will gain confidence. This will lead to more success.

Set aside time to talk about goal-setting with your child. Talk about your goals and encourage him to talk about his. If your child says he wants to do well in school because then he can become president, or go to college, or the like, you should support these ambitions, without making them goals that should motivate your child to get through difficult days at school. Long-term goals are interesting to talk about, but they can't give your child the immediate feedback and sense of accomplishment and success that he needs and that he can gain through attaining his daily short-term goals.

The more often your child is able to meet the goals he sets, the more motivated he will become. For this reason, you should oversee the goals he sets to be sure they are short-term, realistic, and, more often than not, attainable.

Discourage: "I will get all A's on my report card."
Encourage: "I will study my spelling words for 15 minutes every night this week so that I will get a good grade on Friday's test."

Discourage: "I won't talk in class all this week."
Encourage: "Today, I won't talk while the teacher is talking."

Discourage: "I'm not going to watch TV anymore; I'm going to spend that time reading."

Encourage: "I'm going to give up a half hour of TV each night so I can spend more time reading."

Success-oriented people set goals for themselves. When they attain them, they set new ones. If they fall short, they adjust their goals and try again. Talk to your child about his goals, write his goals down each day, and let him check them off when they are accomplished. If they are not reached, don't be disappointed or angry; help him to adjust them if necessary and then encourage him to try again.

Goal-setting can break down school work into manageable pieces. For 8-year-old Josh, this made the difference between remaining an unhappy, average student and becoming a competent, happy one. Josh wanted to do well in school, but hard as he tried, he couldn't get the good grades that he wanted. Every time he brought home a test paper with a C or a D grade, he felt angry and defeated. He used to promise his parents that next time he would get all A's, but now he just apologizes for being stupid. Josh's parents also wanted him to do well in school, but it was obvious to them that something was going wrong somewhere between Josh's good intentions and his performance. They decided that before they too threw up their hands and conceded that Josh just didn't have it in him to be an A student, they would try something a friend had suggested.

They decided to help Josh set attainable goals that would teach him how to get ready for tests and would give him a sense of accomplishment along the way. "Even if he doesn't get A's," they reasoned, "he'll at least learn how to study."

Each day Josh and his parents wrote down a goal and each night they would talk about it and check it off if it was accomplished. The first few days looked like this:

Day 1: I will go to class prepared. I will remember to bring all my books and homework papers with me to school. ✓

Day 2: I will go to class prepared. ✓
     I will raise my hand to answer questions I know the answers to. ✓

Day 3: I will go to class prepared. ✓
     I will raise my hand to answer questions. ✓

I will put answers on the blackboard if my teacher asks for volunteers. ✓

Josh's parents encouraged him to repeat goals from previous days in the hope of developing good work habits. They also helped him add new goals that they felt would help Josh pay closer attention in class. Josh's parents trusted him to tell them the truth about reaching in-school goals that they could not personally observe. (You might want to check with the teacher if you have any reason to doubt that the goals are really being met.) After only one week of short-term goal setting, Josh earned an A on his science test. As the weeks went on and Josh continued to set and meet goals, all of his grades improved.

Like many families, Josh and his parents were about ready to resign themselves to average work. But when Josh gained a sense of competence through short-term and realistic goal-setting, he was motivated to continue to organize his study skills in ways that helped him get the grades he wanted.

State Positive Expectations

You can motivate your child to do his best in school by making positive expectations the standard in your home. Always express in your conversations and your attitude: "Of course we do our best when we work. Is there any other way?"

You begin to instill this attitude in your children by modeling it in your own behavior. When you find yourself faced with a difficult or unpleasant task, talk out loud about how you feel and let your child watch you see it through to a successful end. For example, Joan was asked by her church group to write a newspaper article about their recent carnival. "When Mr. Henderson asked me to do this," she told her daughter Stephanie, "I was really worried that I wouldn't be able to do a good job. But then when I thought about it, I realized, 'Why not? I can write as well as anyone else on the publicity committee.' So I did it and I think it sounds very good. Listen; what do you think?" Joan then read the article to her daughter. She didn't really need Stephanie's opinion, but she wanted her to realize that facing a challenge with a positive attitude makes it more likely that you'll do well.

Most children will be influenced by the level of expectation that is placed before them. That's why it is not unusual to hear parents of C students say, "My child doesn't really like school. But that's okay as long as he brings home at least C's." That's what they expect; that's what they get. It's important, of course, to know your child's abilities and limitations when setting grade expectations (see Chapter 2 for a full discussion of aptitude), but grades are not the whole ball of educational wax. All students, whether learning disabled or gifted, hyperactive or withdrawn, will rise to meet consistent positive expectations concerning such basic things as: paying attention in class, doing homework, studying for tests, and going to school prepared. These things are not dependent on a child's IQ; they are work habits that all children need in order to do their personal best.

You cannot *make* your child do well in school. But you can motivate him to *want* to do well. Try all of the positive motivators explained in this chapter. Then zero in on the ones that seem to work best for you and your child. If, after consistently using positive motivators, your child still will not try to do well in school, you may have to move on to the program of penalties that follows. This program will teach your child that there are family rules about doing school work and there is a price to pay for breaking these rules. If you use this penalty approach, be sure you use it in combination *with* the positive motivators described thus far.

Penalties

Sometimes penalties can be used to motivate children to do their best in school. But don't jump into punishments at the first sign of a problem. First try using social and concrete rewards consistently for one month. If at the end of that month you find that your child is still not doing what he needs to do to be successful in school, it's time to set up a penalty system.

Setting up a Penalty System

If they are to stay within established guidelines, all people need to know where the limits are set. As a parent, you should not suddenly decide, "That's it! I've had it! You've pushed me too far! Now you're going to get it!" An effective penalty system is one set up in advance. Limits and rules are discussed and established. And consequences for breaking the rules are determined. *Before* you decide to use penalties to change your child's behavior, sit down and explain to him exactly what you expect from him and what will happen if he doesn't meet your expectations. When you do this, follow these guidelines:

Make It Specific:

Focus on exactly what is keeping your child from doing his best in school. If you can't change these behaviors with positive rewards, then it's time to lay down the law and stand firm. Make the rule as specific as possible. This will give your child a secure framework that leaves no doubts about what is expected from him. You should not say, for example, "You must be good in school." Instead say, "You can talk during playtime and at lunch time, but you must not talk when the teacher expects you to be listening or working."

Make It Reasonable:

Your rules should also be reasonable; your child should be physically and developmentally able to follow them. Sometimes parents set rules in anger that are impossible for children to obey. A rule, for example, that tells a 6-year-old "You must read for two hours every night" will overwhelm the child with frustration because 6-year-olds can't do *anything* for two hours straight. Make your rules reasonable and you'll find that your children are more likely to comply with them.

Make It Enforceable:

Before you make a rule, make sure you can enforce it. Ask yourself if you will be able to follow through on the promised consequence *every* time the rule is broken, and also if you will always know when the rule is broken. Do not set formal rules about classroom behavior ("You must listen when your teacher is talking") unless you know you'll be able to talk to the teacher each day. Do not set rules about after-school activities ("Do not do your homework with the TV on") unless you or a trusted adult will be there to see that they're followed. Do not threaten a penalty that you don't want to enforce ("If you fail one more test, you're off the baseball team"). Think before you make a rule. If you should slip and make one that is not reasonable or enforceable, admit your mistake and try again with a new one. There's nothing to gain by standing firm on a rule that you know isn't going to work effectively.

Give a Reason:

Tell your child *why* he must follow the rules you set. Even when the reason seems quite obvious to you, your child may honestly not know why, for example, he has to study for his test. Also, when you explain the reasoning behind a rule, you sound logical rather than bossy, and this alone increases the likelihood of compliance. When you take the time to explain the reason for a rule, you will also foster your child's growing sense of self-discipline. Children gain a stronger degree of internal motivation when they clearly understand why something is good for them.

Enforce Consistently and Immediately:

Once rules are firmly established, many children will obey them simply because they know and understand them. These external limits help children to develop an internal sense of self-discipline. However, if your child breaks a rule that was set up in advance with the consequence for breaking it built right into the rule, he has made a decision to take the penalty. Don't let him down. Don't give him one more chance to do what he knows is expected of him, and don't let any time lapse between breaking the rule and enforcing the consequence. The "wait-till-your-father-gets-home" school of discipline will not improve your child's school work. Whoever (mom or dad) is there when the rule is broken must follow through on its enforcement. And the other parent should not repeat the penalty when he or she comes home. Once is enough.

You must also enforce the rule every time it's broken. It's very confusing to a child who is trying to learn how to behave when sometimes an action is ignored and other times it is punished. Enforce the rules whenever they are broken no matter how busy you are or who's around.

Kinds of Penalties

Penalties are the unpleasant things that happen to your child if he breaks a family rule. Unpleasant things that can encourage your child to improve his school work include a brief scolding, the loss of a privilege or possession, and being forced to learn the hard way.

A Brief Scolding:

We said earlier that you can teach your child to do well in school without yelling. So a brief "scolding" may sound like a contradiction—but it is not. This scolding penalty is not the same as yelling. It is a brief (no more than one minute) discussion that gives you time to explain to your child:

- What is wrong: "Your teacher told me that you are still clowning around, jumping out of your seat, and talking back to her."
- Why it is wrong: "This makes your teacher angry because she can't teach the rest of the class if she has to continually stop to ask you to behave. She also knows that you're not

learning as well as you could when you're not paying attention."
- What will happen the next time: "If you misbehave like this again tomorrow, you will not be allowed to play with your friends after school. You'll come right home and help me clean the house."
- What your child should be doing instead: "While you're in the classroom you must sit in your seat, keep your mouth closed unless you're answering a question, and talk nicely to your teacher."

You should finish the scolding by making sure your child understands what he did wrong. Ask him to tell you why he's being scolded. Then re-establish the affectionate bonds between the two of you. Let him know you still love him and you know that if he tries, tomorrow will be a better day at school.

These steps can be covered in less than one minute. Once the scolding is finished—drop it! Don't begin to lecture, yell, or threaten. The purpose of a brief scolding is to show your disappointment and to teach your child how to change his negative actions into acceptable behaviors. Use an assertive tone of voice with a stern look on your face, but don't drag it out or raise your voice. If your child does not change his behavior after the scolding, he knows what will happen. Be sure to follow through and enforce one of the following penalties.

Loss of a Privilege or Possession:

This penalty says to your child, "If you do not follow the rules, you will lose something that you like." That "something" may include use of the TV or video games, outside playtime, a favorite toy, or the right to use the telephone.

If you decide to use this penalty, make sure that the loss is unpleasant and realistically enforceable. If it's not, it won't help your child do well in school. If you take away your child's right to play video games until he brings home a passing grade on Wednesday's spelling test, for example, this won't encourage him to study if he is allowed to go to his friend's house where he can play video games all afternoon. Or, if you take away your child's right to use the telephone for one month because he talked back to his teacher, you will probably give in after only a few days because it's tough to enforce *any* penalty for such a long period of time. When you back down, no lesson is learned. On the other hand, if you do stand firm and keep your child off the phone for the entire month, he will soon forget why he can't use the phone, so it won't change his behavior, and he will begin to see you as the bad guy who holds a grudge.

When you decide to take away a privilege or possession, make sure it's an enforceable loss, do it for a reasonable period of time, and make sure your child understands the connection between the loss and his actions.

Learning the Hard Way:

You can sometimes teach your child to take responsibility for his school work by doing nothing to stop him from getting into trouble. When you do this, natural consequences will teach your child that if he breaks a rule, you will not be there to help him out of the jam and he will have to live with the results. (You cannot use this, of course, if the consequence would be physically harmful to your child or to others in any way.)

School situations that might be best handled with natural consequences include:

"Do your homework *now*. If you're not finished by 8:00, you'll have to go to school tomorrow without it."

"You have a project due next Friday; I think you should start on it now. If you wait until Thursday night to start, don't look to me for help."

"You have to get all your school things organized in one place each night so you don't leave books and papers at home. If you do leave things home, I'm not going to bring them to school for you."

The most difficult part of letting your child learn the hard way is actually following through and letting him face the consequences. It's very difficult to let our children go to school unprepared, or to refuse to help them when they get themselves in a bind. So be sure to use this penalty *only* when you're fully prepared to follow through. Then if your child does have to face the negative consequences of his actions, your job is done. Don't scold, nag, or yell. The point is to let your child learn the lesson for himself.

Rewards and Penalties In Action

• Christine was forgetful. She could not remember what she needed to bring home from school, what she should bring back to school, or when long-term assignments were due. Her parents were tired of running around behind her reminding her of what she needed, driving her back to school to get forgotten materials, bringing homework to her at school, and working with her through the night just before a project was due. Her parents decided that it was time for Christine to take responsibility for herself, and so they set up this rule:

RULE: "Christine, you must remember the things you need to do well in school."

REASON: "We won't always be around to look after you and remind you of your responsibilities. It's important that you learn to take care of yourself."

POSITIVE CONSEQUENCE: "We will help you organize your home study aids. We will buy you a large calendar so you can write down what's due. When you remember to bring home all your supplies for four days in a row (as marked on your progress chart), you may have two friends over for a pizza dinner."

NEGATIVE CONSEQUENCE: "We will no longer drive back to school to get your materials. We will not deliver your things to you at school, and we will not help you do projects at the last minute. You will have to live with the problems that occur when you forget things."

Christine's parents hoped that this active guidance, promise of a reward, and fear of the natural consequence of her forgetfulness would teach her to organize her materials and her work. The first two days after setting the rule, Christine brought everything home that she needed. Her work was organized and complete. Then on the third day, she left her homework assignment pad in school. She begged her mom to take her back for it. Her mom reminded her of the rule and ignored the next three hours of crying and complaining. During the following week, Christine began to remember her things. There were still days when she felt the rule was cruel and unfair, but her parents stood firm. They praised their daughter's success and ignored her failures. Within two weeks they were happy to see that the successes far outnumbered the failures. Three weeks after setting the rule, Christine and two friends had a celebration pizza party.

› Jake was an 11-year-old student who didn't care much for school. But he did his classwork and passed his tests with C's and B's. When he brought home his first marking period report card, his parents were surprised to see an F for "Homework Assignments." They had checked Jake's homework every night and they had helped him with some of the difficult assignments. What they didn't know was that Jake would often lie about how much homework he had.

When Jake's teacher explained what appeared to be happening his parents asked her to call them any day that Jake did not bring in all of his homework. Then they set up the following penalty system:

RULE: "You must do all of your homework every night."

REASON: "Your homework will help you understand your lessons better and it is your responsibility to do whatever work your teacher assigns."

POSITIVE CONSEQUENCE: "I will call your teacher every day. If she tells me that you brought in completed homework assignments, you can stay outside and play for an extra half hour at night."

NEGATIVE CONSEQUENCE: "If your teacher tells us that you did not bring in an assignment, you will not be allowed to play outside with your friends that day at all."

Jake's parents hoped that the promise of extra play time and the fear of losing his right to play with his friends would push him to do his work. They were right. Jake's teacher never had to call with bad news and they were able to praise his honesty and hard work each day. On the next report card, not only did Jake earn an A in "Homework Assignments," but some of his subject grades went up as well. Apparently, Jake just needed to know that it is not acceptable to lie and skimp on homework.

- Each night 12-year-old Nina would sit down to do her homework. Her parents would cross their fingers and hope that she would finish quickly before the battle began. Most often, Nina would jump up from her homework table two minutes after she started, and run off to do something else that was more fun. The moment Nina's mom took her eyes off her, she was gone—gone off to play with her friends, gone to watch TV or to talk on the phone. Her mom spent most nights searching for Nina and then dragging her back to the homework table to try again. "If you keep it up," her mother would shout, "I'm going to tie you to that chair!" Of course, her mother never intended to follow through on this threat, but she had already tried begging and hollering. Now she didn't know what else to do. Finally one night Nina's parents decided on the following rule:

RULE: "You must sit down at the homework table and stay there for 20 minutes. Then you can take a 10-minute break. And then it's back to the homework table until your homework is finished."

REASON: "You have to do homework. You can't learn anything if you won't stay put. Also, I have my own work to do and I don't want to chase you around all night."

POSITIVE CONSEQUENCE: "If you sit still for each 20-minute period, you will get your work done faster and have more time to do what you want. Each night that you follow this rule, you may talk on the phone or watch TV for an extra 20 minutes."

NEGATIVE CONSEQUENCE: "You will lose one half hour of TV watching time whenever you get up from the table during homework time."

The first night Nina jumped up and ran off after doing her homework for only 5 minutes. Her mother brought her back, reminded her that she had just lost one half hour of TV time. After Nina stopped complaining, her dad reminded her that she would lose another half hour if she got up again before the 20 minutes was over. Nina sat still for the rest of her homework time, but she became very upset when her parents turned off the TV a half hour early that night. The next night, Nina sat still for the entire 20-minute period, and then watched an extra 20 minutes of TV. Her parents expect that she will forget and jump up again someday soon, but they're not worried because now they know how to handle it when it happens.

Physical Punishment

Do not, at any point, resort to physical punishment. Spanking, hitting, slapping, whipping, beating, etc., do not encourage children to develop self-control. And that, after all, is the goal in your involvement in your child's education. Instead, you may find that physical punishment will make your child angry, hostile, and fearful. And it will teach him that violence is an acceptable way to handle problems.

A recent *Time* magazine article reported that in Cobb County, Georgia, police have reviewed accounts of child abuse for a two-year period and found that reports of abuse as much as double in the three days after school grades are issued. Because some parents do use physical punishment to "motivate" their children to do better school work, child-welfare groups and educators in several areas are mounting public-education campaigns aimed at stopping the "report-card reflex." The programs, modeled after a similar plan begun in Houston by the Child Abuse Prevention Council, use newspaper ads, TV and radio announcements, school fliers mailed to students' homes, and brochures inserted into report cards. All these materials contain the same basic message for parents: Raising voices or fists is *not* the answer to raising grades.[4]

As you can see from the examples we've noted, using penalties to change your child's behavior does not mean you have to yell, hit, or threaten; there are alternatives. Penalties should always be administered in a firm, matter-of-fact manner. Stand resolute without losing your cool. Follow through with the promised consequence, and remind your child that he has chosen to face the penalty. When it's over, don't hold a grudge. Let your child know that he does not lose your love when he breaks a rule. He must learn to pay the price of his actions—life is like that.

If this penalty system is used consistently as described and your child still does not change his actions, re-evaluate the penalty you're using. Remember, penalties must be unpleasant to the child, yet reasonable and enforceable. Maybe you need to try something else.

What makes a child *want* to do well in school? Most parents can make their children do well enough by pushing them through assignment after assignment and grade level after grade level. But your involvement in your child's education should not be based on a "Do well today because I say so" philosophy. It should exist to foster your child's sense of self-discipline and self-direction so that he will achieve on his own because he enjoys feeling accomplished and competent. This kind of inner motivation is not born in children—it has to be learned. Think carefully about what you want to teach your child, then choose the method of positive and/or negative motivation that will best do the job.

Resource List

Books

- *Between Parent and Child*
  Haim Ginott
  Avon, 1976
- *Discipline Without Shouting or Spanking*
  Jerry Wyckoff and Barbara Unell
  Meadowbrook, 1984
- *How to Influence Children*
  Charles E. Schaefer
  Van Nostrand Reinhold, 1982
- *P.E.T.-Parent Effectiveness Training*
  Thomas Gordon
  New American Library, 1988
- Teach Your Child to Behave
  Charles E. Schaefer
  New American Library, 1990

Video Cassette

- *Mirror*
  Keebler/National PTA
  This video emphasizes the role of family communication in building a can-do attitude in school-age children. ($20) Write *Mirrors*, 500 N. Michigan Avenue, Suite 200 M, Chicago, Illinois 60611.

5

"Whose homework is this, anyway?"

The Parent's Role/The Child's Role and Getting the Work Done

Janet often complains, "If I don't push Erin through every step of her homework, it just doesn't get done." One of her friends nods in agreement. "Jason answers a few questions every night, then says, 'I don't know how to do the rest.' So, of course, I end up doing them for him just to get it over with." Another parent adds, "Jackie tells me she never has homework, but I wonder if that's true."

In theory homework is a simple concept. It's school work that is taken out of the classroom and worked on at home. In reality, however, homework is much more complex. If you bring up the topic the next time you're chatting with your kids, or their friends, or other parents, you'll probably find that homework is not on the top of the "Things I Love to Do" list for most people. Why is that? Very young school children usually enjoy having homework; in fact, if they don't have any, they pretend that they do. What happens to their enthusiasm? Where does that love of learning, exploring, and accomplishment go?

This chapter will help you maintain or re-create your child's (and your own) positive attitude toward homework. It will clarify *why* homework is valuable, define your role and your child's in getting the work done, and offer solutions to specific homework problems. Homework is one aspect of education that gives you an opportunity for direct, concrete input. Grab hold of it and use it to help your child find success in school.

Homework Is Good for Kids

Negative attitudes are often voiced the loudest when the subject of homework comes up in conversation. Some parents don't like homework because it interferes with their family routines, takes too much time from days that are already several hours too short, and is a constant source of conflict with their children. Many children hate homework because it takes time away from other things that they like. Even teachers sometimes don't give homework because it's bothersome and some aren't sure if it's really helpful. Despite these feelings, many people believe homework is a good thing. In fact, for two decades the annual Gallup poll of the public's attitude toward the public schools has found that the majority of people in this country favor the continued practice of assigning homework and support increasing the amount of homework given to children of all ages. A few facts that may have influenced these beliefs and that are generally supported by educational experts follow. Read them over and see for yourself that homework does more than annoy kids with boring work.

- Homework improves school grades. A recent study found that when low-ability students do just one to three hours of homework a week, their grades are usually as high as those of average-ability students who do no homework at all. And when average-ability students do three to five hours of homework a week, their grades are usually equal to those of high-ability students who do no homework.
- Homework gives children the time they need to fit new facts into their already established set of knowledge.
- Homework fosters the ability to work independently.
- Homework reinforces daily school lessons—a key factor in learning.
- Homework enables children to build lifelong work habits of budgeting time independently, organizing materials, and doing the job.
- Homework builds self-discipline by requiring that a child put his attention to the work at hand despite distractions. This gives a child the habit of persistence in the face of difficulties.

Homework is good for parents too:

- Homework gives you an opportunity to enrich your child's school work by personalizing it to his needs and interests. You can use his love of baseball, for example, to explain the word "velocity." And you can use her love of underwater swimming to illustrate the body's use of oxygen.
- Homework allows you insight into areas of learning where your child needs individualized help.
- Homework is an invaluable communication link between you and your child's school. It helps you understand what your child is learning, the quality of the educational materials he is using, and some of the teaching methods being used.

Whose Homework Is This?

Most elementary-school children need help with their homework. There's a great deal of disagreement, however, over exactly what "help" means. What kind of helper are you:

- Do you work step-by-step with your children through each assignment?
- Do you step in whenever there's a problem?
- Do you check it over only when it's all finished?
- Do you fix mistakes?
- Do you "enhance" school projects by doing the work yourself?

Whatever your answers, you must decide if your approach is helping or hurting your child. Keeping in mind that the ultimate value of doing homework is to develop an *independent* work habit and to foster *self*-discipline, re-think the way you presently get involved and then divide up the homework responsibilities in this way:

Child: The one who must *do* the homework.
Parent: The one who must see that homework gets done by the child. Also, the one who must *motivate, show interest in,* and *encourage* the child.

Once you have your roles clearly defined, you can start to help your child do his work.

How You Can Help

Homework is a part of education that your child will have to deal with for the rest of his school years. That's why you want to find a way to help your child get the assignments done and get the most out of them in ways that are the best for both of you *in the long run.* A popular short-term method that pushes children through assignments involves screaming at the child and using threats. Some parents might say for example, "Do your homework now or you'll get a smack and then I'll throw out the TV." That may get the job done for tonight—but what will it take tomorrow night? Your job is to oversee your child's work in ways that will build the kind of study habits that will eventually phase you out of the picture and that will support the goals of establishing independent work habits and self-sufficiency.

To do this you'll need to invest some time in conveying to your child the value of homework. This is an investment that will pay you back eventually with more peaceful, less time-consuming homework periods. *You* know that homework teaches valuable work habits, but this fact won't impress your child because it doesn't give him immediate feedback. Therefore, look for practical value in homework assignments. Tell your child that his lesson in subtraction will help him make sure he gets the right change when he buys gum at the store, that his lesson in writing will help him write a letter to his grandma, and that his reading assignment will help him read his baseball cards. Whenever possible, find a valuable and practical reason for the assigned work. (Read more about this in Chapter 9.)

Then, put down your whistle, megaphone, and stopwatch and enlist your child's help in setting up a homework routine. Children have a more positive attitude toward work when they have some input and control over the circumstances. This also shifts the responsibility for doing homework back to the child (where it belongs) and it gives him a greater sense of independent accomplishment when he sets his own rules. (We'll discuss how to establish when and where to do homework later in the chapter.)

Finally, establish your role as a homework consultant, rather than a homework doer. Let your child know that you will clarify instructions, give example solutions, note mistakes, listen to his math facts, quiz him on his spelling words, help him learn how to study, point the way to the textbook, encyclopedia, or reference work that contains the correct answer. Then make it clear that you will not fill in the answers, fix the mistakes, or look up needed information. You may find that *not* doing your child's homework is not easy, but in the long run it will be easiest and best for both of you.

Support Good Study Habits

How do habits get started? They usually form when a person does something in the same way, at the same time, and in the same place over and over and over until he or she does it automatically without effort or forethought. You can help your child develop good study habits by helping him choose *where, when,* and *how* to study, and by encouraging him to use the selected schedule and method *every* school day. (Make exceptions only in the most dire circumstances.) One day, you'll notice that the routine has turned into a habit—your child will sit down at the appointed time and place, open his books and begin to work without your prodding, coaxing, or pushing. On that day you'll know he has a most valuable educational tool—an independent work habit.

Where to Work

Ideally, each child has a quiet study place that is comfortable and free of distractions, well lit, and properly equipped with a student-size desk, chair, and supplies. If you do not already have such a place for your child, create one. Which room in your home has a table and chair, is properly lit, and is most free of such distractions as TV, stereo, siblings, telephone? Make that room the homework place. Clear the area of all miscellaneous distractions—toys, comics, radio, magazines, baseball cards, jewelry box, etc. Supply the homework place with paper, pen, pencils, pencil sharpener, ruler, dictionary and other needed reference books. Make that area (be it in the kitchen or dining room, the hallway, or the bedroom) the homework place. Make it clear that each day's homework must be done only in that place.

When to Work

There is no pat answer to the question, "Should children do homework right after school or should they wait until after supper?" The best time is when the homework place is quietest and most free from distractions. It's also whatever time maximizes your child's willingness to work. To decide when homework should be done, consider your child's preference, the time it usually takes to complete assignments, and the family's work and play schedule.

Different children work best on different schedules. Some like to get homework done right after school so they are then free to play outside and watch TV without being interrupted. Other children need a break after school and are more willing to work after they've had a chance to play and have dinner first. Still others (especially those with short attention spans) prefer to work a little after school, stop for some play and dinner, and then finish before bedtime. Ask your child when he wants to do homework. Help him decide by talking over your work schedule, his play schedule (sports, scouting, free time, etc.), and family obligations (doctor appointments, shopping trips, etc.). Pick the time that's most convenient for everyone and then stick to it. Consistency is the most important element in developing study habits, so make sure that homework is done at the same time and in the same place every day.

If your young child doesn't have homework, you can still begin to build homework habits by setting aside a special time and place every day to talk about school and to review the day's lessons. If your older child doesn't have homework every day, insist that he go to his special place at the scheduled time for a short review of the day's work or for some extra reading time. This will lessen his temptation to skip homework in favor of more playtime, and it will also maintain the habit of doing some school work at home every day.

If your child usually does his homework after school at a friend's house or while being supervised by a babysitter, you and your child and his care-giver should sit down and decide exactly when and where homework will be done each day. If possible, call your child during this homework period to ask how he's doing, to encourage his efforts, and to compliment him on getting the work done. Then set a scheduled time when you will meet with your child after dinner to go over the homework and help him find the answers to difficult problems. If it sometimes happens that your child is in bed when you arrive home, arrange one place where homework can be left out for you to review it. If you can't discuss the assignment before school the next morning, be sure to leave an encouraging note saying something like, "I'm proud you did this by yourself," or, "This looks terrific. Ask your teacher to help you re-work number 5."

Scheduling exactly when and where homework is to be done each day makes it easier for kids to get started. It eliminates the need for your child to make daily decisions such as, "Should I start my homework now or play with my friends?" "Should I do my homework in the kitchen or on my bed?" "Should I work with the TV on or off?" You can help him follow the schedule by writing down your agreement on a sign like this:

Homework Time: 7:00 P.M.
Homework Place: The kitchen table
Signed: _____   _____
          child   parent

Have your child sign the agreement and then hang it where he can see it easily. It will serve as a constant reminder, a piece of silent motivation, and will lessen the need for nagging reminders.

You cannot force your children to pay attention to the work in front of them, but you can arrange the conditions and the environment of their workplace in ways that will increase their ability and desire to pay attention.

Motivate!

Parents who begin this homework schedule with a young child who is still anxious to do school work find that good work habits form quite easily and usually last throughout their years of schooling. Like other daily habits, such as brushing teeth and washing hands, if your child knows the task is not negotiable nor flexible, he will do it with little resistance. If, however, your child already has a negative attitude toward homework and has developed some bad work habits, you'll need to offer him some incentive to change his approach to studying. Parents who try to encourage good work habits with threats of punishment and loss of privileges find that they must wage the same verbal battle every night. They also find that if the work does get done, it is often done sloppily and haphazardly. This happens because anger excites the emotions and interferes with learning; anger is also an incentive for defiance. Instead, use a reward system to give reluctant children the initial positive reinforcement they need to get into the homework habit without complaint. (Positive reinforcement is explained in detail in Chapter 4.)

A complete change of work habits doesn't happen in one day. Your child will probably test your determination to change the status quo. Expect complaints; then you won't be thrown off guard. Plan ahead to ignore the obstacles ("I forgot my book") and momentary regressions ("I forgot you said I couldn't watch TV when I do homework"). Instead, concentrate on offering praise, encouragement, and positive feedback. Tell your child that you're happy to see he remembered that it is homework time. Comment on his ability to work without the stereo. Don't wait for him to have the entire routine down perfect before you offer a compliment; praise every effort to do well.

Positive attention from you is a powerful motivator. It's all that some children need to maintain interest in good study habits. Other children, however, may need more concrete rewards as incentive to do homework. Think of the things that your child likes and then find ways to use them in a positive way. Although most parents are quite adept at saying, "If you don't finish this assignment you can't watch TV tonight," this only serves to make children angry and resentful. Changing this punishment into a privilege is merely a matter of wording. Instead, say, "You can watch TV tonight when you finish all your homework." This gives your child incentive to work toward a privilege. As you support your child in his efforts to do his homework, practice this skill of positive wording. Catch yourself before you threaten, "You can't . . . until . . ." and change it to, "You can . . . when you . . ."

Homework Gremlins

Even after the homework habit is established in your household, you may find that your child has a specific problem that interferes with his ability to get all his work done. You may notice that your child:

* doesn't bring home his books.
* doesn't know what the homework assignment is, or insists he doesn't have any.
* whines and complains about doing homework.
* does sloppy and/or careless work.
* wants constant attention and help. He won't work alone.
* takes an unusually long time to complete homework assignments.

The following section of this chapter will help you find solutions to these problems while you continue to maintain a fixed time and place homework schedule.

Problem:

"I forgot my books."

Ten-year-old Bobby often sits down in his special home-work place at the agreed-upon homework time and then realizes that he doesn't have the books he needs to do his assignments. When this happens, Bobby either decides to skip the assignment, or he calls a friend hoping to get the information he needs. When he skips the assignment, Bob-by's forgetfulness causes him to earn poor grades. When he calls a friend, he wastes time, gets distracted by social phone conversation, and most often finds he can't do the work without the book and so asks his friend to give him just the answers. In this case, Bobby is learning that it is easier to forget his books and take credit for other people's work.

Remedy:

If your child, like Bobby, is forgetful, you need to find out *why* he forgets to bring home the things he needs.

- Is he in a hurry at the end of each day to catch the school bus? If so, explain the situation to his teacher and ask if he can have an extra 60 seconds of class time at the end of each school day to get his things together.
- Is he in a hurry to get out of school to play with his friends? If so, he needs to be motivated with positive reinforcers like those described in Chapter 2 to take the time necessary to carefully gather his things together. For example, you should praise your child and show approval every time he remembers his books. If he only remembers to bring home one out of three needed books, praise him for remember-ing the one and convey your belief that the next time he'll remember them all. Offer a concrete reward (like a special snack, or extra time on the telephone) when he remembers to bring home everything he needs. Once he gets into the habit of thinking about his assignments before he leaves school, you can gradually phase out the rewards (but con-tinue to give praise!).

- Is your young child forgetting books because there is simply too much to remember at the end of each school day? It's difficult for a young child to remember a coat, hat, book bag, lunch box, notebook, spelling book, etc. Children up to the age of 8 may not be able to remember everything without some help. Talk with your child's teacher; explain the problem and ask him or her to assist your child in gathering his supplies together. If the problem persists or if the teacher is unable to help, you might ask if you can keep an extra set of books at home. Some school administrators will allow this arrangement when the parents explain that it's a necessity not a luxury. Although your goal is to develop independent work habits in your child, some children (especially those who are generally disorganized and forgetful) need this extra help in order to put their powers of concentration on the assignment itself.

- Is your child forgetting his books because he's found it easier to get the answers from friends? Or, does he feel it lessens his responsibility when he can say, "I want to do my homework, but I can't because I don't have the book I need"? When true forgetfulness isn't the problem, you can handle the "I forgot my book" dilemma as you would any other discipline problem:

1. *Set a rule:* "You must bring home everything you need to do your homework assignments because without the proper supplies you can't meet your school responsibilities."
2. *Set a positive consequence:* "When you do bring home your books, your school grades will improve; I will be proud of you, and you will earn a star on the Progress Chart. (See page 85 for a sample chart.) When you have four stars in a row, you can have your friend sleep overnight."
3. *Set a negative consequence:* "If you forget your books again, I will not drive you back to school to get them." If you can't do that, consider consequences such as taking away TV watching for the evening or adding an extra 15 minutes of reading time to the homework period to make up the time taken away from the subject work he can't do. To avoid the negative consequences of forgetting, some children will claim, "I don't have any homework." Don't let your child think that you are easily fooled. Let him know that you will check with the teacher the next day.

Problem:

"I forget what I have to do." Or, "I don't have any homework, again."

Seven-year-old Janet often sits at her homework desk with all her books spread out in front of her and stares at the wall in bewilderment. She hasn't a clue as to what she's supposed to do. When the assignment was given by the teacher, Janet listened carefully and felt she understood what she had to do. Once home, however, she couldn't remember. Other nights, Janet tells her parents she doesn't have any homework, when in fact she does but she has forgotten all about it.

Remedy:

If your child forgets what to do for homework, he needs a memory aid. Buy him a small assignment notebook. Show him how to record the subject and the assignment each day. (If your child is too young to write down the assignment, ask the teacher to do it for him.) Praise him when he records his assignments and encourage him when he forgets.

If the forgetting problem persists or if your child claims he has no homework (when you know he does as indicated by his teacher or the report card), engage the help of the teacher. Explain the problem and ask him or her to check the accuracy of your child's homework pad and initial it each day. If, in fact, there is no homework assignment, the teacher can write that on the pad. Eventually, your child will get into the habit of automatically writing down assignments and you can phase out the teacher's help.

Problem:

"I don't want to."

Nine-year-old Jeff can never get through a day's homework assignment without moaning, groaning, grumbling, sighing, whining, and/or crying. He knows when, where, and how to do his homework, but he just doesn't want to.

Remedy:

If your child consistently shows a keen dislike of homework, try to find out why. Is your child frustrated because he doesn't have the basic skills he needs to do the work? Sit down, give him your undivided attention, and work with him through one night's entire assignment. When the work is finished, ask yourself, "Was he able to understand the directions?" "Was he able to work through the steps of a problem and come up with a reasonable answer?" "Was he willing to try to complete the work?" "Does the assignment seem to be reinforcement of school work rather than brand new concepts?" If you can answer "Yes" to these questions, your child's reason for disliking homework is most likely not an inability to do the work, but rather lack of interest (as explained a little later). If you answer "No" to two or more of these questions, most likely your child dislikes homework because the work is too difficult for him. (We all dislike things that make us feel like a failure.) If that's the case, you should speak to your child's teacher, explain the problem, and work together to find a solution. You might find that your child needs remedial work, or supplemental school instruction, or an individualized program, or private tutoring. When a child hasn't had a chance to grasp basic concepts, the following work that builds on those concepts causes the child to feel more and more frustrated. Most often this problem won't correct itself. As soon as possible, work with the teacher to strengthen your child's base of knowledge.

Is your child groaning over homework assignments because there are too many other things he'd rather be doing? If that's the case you can sometimes ease the "pain" by helping him turn so-called boring assignments into interesting and personalized challenges. Use the information in the section of Chapter 7 called "Encourage Active Studying" and also the suggestions in Chapter 10 to help your child enjoy learning. These sections will show you how to liven up a lesson. If, for example, your child is moaning because he has to read an article about "stupid" worms, you might bring him to a nearby plot of dirt and help him start digging. Bring a worm home, set it in a bowl on the homework table, and help your child relate the information in the article to his live specimen.

Obviously you can't always jazz up dull lessons, but you can reduce the nightly wails of woe by giving positive feedback for every attempt your child makes to work without complaining and, at the same time, by completely ignoring any groaning, whining, mumbling, etc. If you make a habit of giving praise and other forms of positive attention to quiet work and no attention at all to noisy work, it won't be long before the noise will decrease. You can also bolster your efforts to make homework time a bit more enjoyable by offering concrete rewards for work well done. Offer, for example, a work break and a special treat if your child works without complaining for 15 minutes. Offer a trip to the movies if homework is done without complaining for four days in a row. (Use a Progress Chart like the one on page 85 to keep track.) It is remarkable how often a hug, a positive remark, and a bowl of pretzels will encourage a child to face his assignments with a positive attitude.

Problem:

"It's good enough."
Seven-year-old Kate doesn't mind doing homework. She sits down every day, zips through all her assignments without a word of complaint, and then runs outside to play. Unfortunately, the work is done carelessly and it looks quite sloppy. "This is not your best work, Kate," her mom often says. "Oh, it's good enough," Kate casually replies. "My teacher doesn't care."

Remedy:

First off, don't confuse poor handwriting ability with sloppiness. Some children don't yet have the refined motor coordination needed to write neatly. True sloppiness is characterized by incomplete, careless, smudged, and/or wrinkled papers. If your child's homework is truly sloppy and/or carelessly done, you should set higher standards. When homework is done well, children experience a sense of pride and accomplishment. On the other hand, when sloppy work is allowed to pass as acceptable, children learn that laziness and poor work habits are good enough for them.

Sometimes children's sloppiness is due to the fact that they hurry through their assignments in an effort to get back to play. If you think that's the case with your child, you can slow him down by establishing a minimum amount of time for each homework session. If your child finishes his work before the time is up, he can review his lessons or read a book, but he must stay at his desk. This will give him the time he needs to do a careful and neat job.

Do not yell at, nag, or threaten your child for doing sloppy work. Instead, look for some piece of neat, careful work and praise it. Encourage your child to continue working to make all his work as well done as that one section. If your child gets positive attention for good work and silence for poor work, he may soon decide to seek more attention by doing his work carefully.

If your child says sloppiness is "okay" with the teacher, don't hesitate to ask for a clarification of what "okay" means. It is possible that the teacher does not collect or give any attention to homework assignments. It's also possible that the teacher puts more emphasis on the completion rather than the quality of homework. Tell the teacher that you would like him or her to work with you in encouraging your child to do neat and careful work. Ask the teacher to follow the same method as you use at home (praising good work, giving the cold shoulder to poor work, and stating expectations of high standards). When your child finds that he can't slide by with careless work and that he gets more

attention for being careful, he will probably rise to meet
your expectations.

If sloppy, careless work continues, it's time for the following disciplinary action:

1. *Set a rule:* "Your homework assignments must be done
   with care. You must use your best handwriting and you
   must answer all the questions in the best way you are
   able."
2. *Set a positive consequence:* "When your homework is done
   carefully, you may have ____." (Fill in a special reward or
   privilege). Or, "You will get a star on the Progress Chart
   [see page 85 for a sample chart] every day that you do
   your homework carefully and neatly. When you have four
   stars in a row, you may have ____." (Fill in a special
   reward or privilege.)
3. *Set a negative consequence:* "When your homework is
   done sloppily, you will not be allowed to ____." (Fill in
   with a loss of privilege such as use of the TV after dinner.)
   Or, "You will have to do the entire assignment over again
   correctly."

Once the rules are established, understood, and agreed
upon, you have no need to nag or badger. Just follow
through each and every day and watch sloppy work habits
turn into ones your child will be proud of.

Problem:

"You have to help me."
Eleven-year-old Brian wants his parents' undivided attention when he does his homework. His mom explains the
assignment, does an example for him, and leaves him to
complete the work. Without fail, within 5 minutes Brian is
standing at her side, book in hand, saying, "I don't understand how to do this." Brian's mom takes him back to his
work place, explains the assignment again, and then leaves.
In a short while Brian is back at her side again, whining that
he cannot do the work. Brian has trouble working independently; he feels lost unless someone guides him through

every step of his work. Over the years, his teachers noticed this problem and had often told his parents that Brian worked best with individualized attention. But now his parents feel it is time for Brian to learn how to work without constant assistance.

Remedy:

The remedy to this problem depends, of course, on the cause. Is it possible that your child really can't do the level of work assigned? When you do give him your undivided attention, does he still appear frustrated and confused? If he does, get in touch with his teacher as soon as possible. Explain the situation and find out exactly how your child can get extra help and individualized remedial attention. If the teacher cannot guarantee any specific program of assistance, meet with the principal and/or the director of special services. Do not let one more year pass without getting your child the help he needs to grasp hold of the basic skills he's lacking. If the school programs do not seem to remedy the problem, you may need to hire a private tutor or, if possible, look into changing schools.

Has your child made a habit of working only in your company and/or of having you do his work for him? If he keeps following you around because he likes to be near you and wants your attention, then it's time to again clarify your role in the homework situation and offer positive attention only when he works independently.

A natural parental reaction to this problem might be, "Get back to your room right now and don't come out again until you've finished the assignment." Unfortunately, this response will only make your child sulk and drag out the homework time with self-pitying mutterings. Instead, try a positive approach. Tell your child that although you can't do his homework for him, you'll be glad to read over his work to be sure it's being done correctly. Tell him that you'll do that after he's worked for 5 minutes straight without getting up from the table or calling for you. Then set a kitchen timer for 5 minutes and tell him you'll be in to check on his progress as soon as the timer rings. If your child calls for you before the time is up, calmly remind him of your agreement and reset the timer for 5 more full minutes and try again. When your child realizes that he will get your attention only when he works by himself, he will do it. When you go to him, be sure to praise him for working independently, check his work, and then set the timer for another 5 minutes. After a day or two of 5-minute stretches between homework checks, change the check-in time to 7 minutes, then to 10, and so on until your child has learned how to work without constant attention.

Problem:

"I'll never finish this."

Six-year-old Andrea has promoted the act of dragging out a homework assignment to an absolute art form. Every day she sits at her homework place and begins her work at the agreed-upon time. Thirty minutes later, when her mom checks in, nothing has been accomplished. "What have you been doing all this time?" her mom always asks. "My homework," says Andrea defensively. "I just didn't get a chance to finish yet." Some nights the work never gets done. Other nights Andrea and her parents spend more time arguing about the problem than it would take simply to do the work. And some days, in the interest of saving time and trouble, Andrea's mom sits down with her daughter and pushes her through the assignments with the air of an efficiency expert, barking, "All right, let's go; move on; what's next; hurry up." None of these approaches have helped Andrea overcome her tendency to dillydally and daydream.

Remedy:

If your child takes what seems like forever to do his homework each night, first check to see if the level of work is too difficult for him to do by himself. When a child doesn't know how to do an assignment (even though he may not admit it to you), he'll sit staring at the wall with no idea where or how to begin. Work through a few assignments with him. Can he tell you one step at a time how to find the answers he needs? Does he seem to understand the basic concepts? Is he able to read and understand the directions? If he can't do these things, you should contact his teacher and, as suggested with the last problem ("You have to help me"), arrange for extra help and individualized remedial assignments.

Some children are able to do the work, but they dilly-dally, daydream, and take a very long time to finish. Some adults too have this problem. They sit down to work with good intentions, but soon need a drink of water, then something to eat. Soon afterward they begin to doodle, write shopping lists, plan for tomorrow's work, and finally surrender to daydreams. The work, of course, remains undone. To encourage your child to get right down to doing his homework, try these suggestions:

- *Schedule the homework period carefully.* Children who tend to dawdle need to do things on an established schedule. Once the homework habit becomes routine, you'll find procrastination problems sharply reduced.

   Schedule the homework period before a fun activity. Let your child know, for example, that when he finishes his homework it will be time to play with his friends, or time to watch TV, etc. This gives your child a reason to keep working until the job is done.
- *Set a manageable goal.* Some children can't get going or keep going because they feel overwhelmed. They don't know where to begin or when it will end. Map out a plan each night that breaks the homework into manageable pieces and gives a time frame for getting the work done. For example, if your child comes home with math, reading, and science homework, focus on just one subject first. Set a kitchen timer for an amount of time in which you think the assignment could be done. Tell him if he finishes the work before the timer goes off (and does it in a neat and acceptable manner), he can take a break and have a reward (a special snack, extra TV time, etc.). Then set a new time schedule and reward for the next assignment and so on until all the work is done.

- *Give reminders.* Every 5 minutes or so during the homework period, remind your child that he should be concentrating on his homework. Don't nag with statements like, "Come on, pay attention." Or, "Stop daydreaming and get that work done." Instead, give your child reminders with positive statements like, "How are you doing?" "Do you need any help?" "Looks like you're doing a good job." These statements will prompt your child to remain focused on the assignment.
- *Let your child pace his work.* If your child has a great deal of trouble sitting still long enough to complete even one assignment (which may indicate a tendency toward hyperactivity), let him work at a work/play pace that will ease the strain of the homework. Try 10 minutes of work and then 10 minutes of play until the homework is completed.
- *Alter your expectations.* Some children are slow moving. They drag out every step of their day from dressing in the morning to undressing at night. That's just the way they are. If you find yourself constantly saying, "Let's go. Hurry up. Get going. Come on; what's the hold up?" You probably need to readjust your expectations. Your child needs more time to do things. Let him dawdle over his homework, but make it clear that there is a limit to the time you are available to help. Set a time, perhaps from 7:00 to 8:00, and say to your child, "I am available to help you during this time; after that, you're on your own." This way your child is free to work at his own pace while you are released from an unending stint of homework duty.

Some children take a very long time to finish their homework because they have to do unfinished classwork at home. If, on a regular basis, your child is doing a great deal of classwork at home, you again need to work closely with his teacher to find out why the work isn't getting done in class. Is the work too difficult for him? Is it too easy and therefore boring? Does he spend too much class time fooling around and daydreaming? Once you find the cause of unfinished assignments, you can begin a program of remedial or accelerated work where appropriate, or when these are not necessary, you can institute a discipline plan as follows:

1. *Set a rule:* "School work must be done in school because that's the proper place to learn your lessons."

2. *Set a positive consequence:* "I am going to talk to your teacher every afternoon. When she tells me that you used your class time for school work, I'll give you _____." (Fill in the blank with a special privilege or reward, like an extra half hour of time for playing video games.)
3. *Set a negative consequence:* "If your teacher tells me that you're still not working in school, you will not be allowed to _____." (Fill in the blank with a privilege like TV watching that will be withheld.)

The key to the effectiveness of this disciplinary action is consistency. Don't say you'll talk to the teacher every day unless you really can do so. Give rewards and penalties *every* day until the habit of concentrating on school work is well established, and remember to praise your child every time he makes an effort to get his work done in school.

Sometimes children take a long time to do their homework because they have a lot of homework to do. If your child is consistently burdened with several hours of homework each night, you should talk to his teacher. There is no hard and fast rule about how much homework is the right amount, but the National PTA and the National Education Association endorse a policy that states, "In the lowest grades—kindergarten to third grade—very little homework should be given, no more than 20 minutes a day. In grades four through six, a child should be expected to spend 20 to 40 minutes a day." These figures will, of course, vary based on the night of the week, the school system, and the grade level, but if you find your elementary-school child working more than one to one and one-half hours each night, he has "too much" work.

Don't give up if the teacher does not agree with your view of "too much" homework. Speak to the school principal and work with members of the school's PTA to investigate the problem and to discuss the possibility of a school-wide homework policy. The National PTA Council suggests that a committee comprised of parents, teachers, and administrators should consider questions such as:

- What is homework supposed to accomplish?
- How can teachers make the best use of homework?
- Should homework be graded and returned?

- Should the school have a formal homework policy that all teachers must abide by?

Homework is a vital part of the educational process. As a parent, you can use it to strengthen the base of your child's growing store of knowledge and to build positive work habits. The next two chapters will show you how to help your children learn test-taking strategies and study skills that will make their work easier, improve their grades, and make them feel better about themselves.

Resource List

Write

- The National PTA
  700 N. Rush Street,
  Chicago, Illinois 60611.
  Ask for the free pamphlet called "Help Your Child Get the Most Out of Homework."

Books

- *Homework Helper: A Guide for Parents Offering Assistance*
  Joan Kuepper
  Education Media Corp., 1987
- *Homework Without Tears*
  Lee Canter and Lee Housner
  Harper and Row, 1988
- *Winning the Homework War*
  Fredric M. Levine and Kathleen M. Anesko
  Prentice-Hall Press, 1987

6

"Did you study for this test?"
Information About Test-taking Strategies and Different Kinds of Tests

Please take notes: At the end of this chapter you will be required to take a test on all the information discussed so far in this book. This isn't true of course, but what if it were? How would you feel? Are you prepared to be evaluated, judged, and compared to other parents who also read this book? Would you welcome the challenge or shy away? Would you go back and study or would you plow ahead and hope you know enough to do well? Do you think a test could fairly judge your ability to help your child do well in school? Will you suffer test anxiety that will cause your mind to go blank?

Regardless of how you feel about the use and value of testing, if you were reading this book as a text in a school-like program, you would probably be required to prove your knowledge by taking a test. Although it is generally agreed by educational experts that it is not an absolute measure of knowledge, testing is the most commonly used means of assessment. Tests are used to diagnose learning problems, measure achievement, learn about students' aptitudes and abilities, and determine final grades that go on permanent records. Many decisions regarding your child's future will be made on the basis of test grades. That's why, for right or wrong, good or bad, your children need to know how to take tests. You can help them prepare for tests, understand how to tackle different types of tests and how to use the results to become a better student.

General Tips

About Cramming

Cramming is a method of studying in which students try to stuff a great deal of information into their short-term memories in a very short period of time. Although time has shown this to be students' favorite method of studying, it is a bad work habit, and it tends to increase test anxiety, interfering with their ability to concentrate. Your child will become a better student if he learns how to budget his study time.

Studying is not a one-shot deal; it's an on-going process that incorporates all class lessons and homework assignments. It is bolstered by a good attendance record and attentive conduct in class. Studying is most effectively done when new material is reviewed each and every day.

Reading Instructions

It is quite common for students to do poorly on tests because they do not listen to and/or read the directions carefully. All classroom teachers have heard students say, "Oh, I didn't know you wanted an essay. I thought you wanted me to list my reasons." "You shouldn't mark these wrong; I didn't know you wanted me to reduce the fractions." "I answered all three questions because I didn't see that we only had to do one. That's why I didn't have time to finish."

Most students will insist that they do read the directions even when the teacher knows they do not. To prove this point, teachers often give out a "test" similar to the one that follows. Make a copy and give it to your older child. If he is like most students, he will waste a lot of time and energy before he realizes his mistake.

PERSONAL INFORMATION FORM

DIRECTIONS: Read over all of the following questions before you answer them. Then fill in the answers as directed.

1. What is your name?
2. How old are you?
3. Do you have any brothers or sisters?
   If so, what are their names and ages?
4. Are your parents married or divorced?
5. What is your mother's maiden name?
6. Do both of your parents work outside the home?
7. Do you like school?
8. What did you eat for breakfast this morning?
9. How would you describe today's weather?
10. Answer question number one; then put your pen down and do not answer any more questions.

Because students often jump immediately into the questions without looking where they're going, many will skip over the direction that instructs them to read all the questions *before* answering. Therefore, they will answer all the questions without knowing that question ten will tell them not to answer numbers two through nine.

Initially, students tend to skip directions because they're in a hurry. Then it becomes a habit. To help your child avoid this trap, watch how he does his homework. Have him read the directions aloud before beginning. Help him get into the habit of carefully reading and following *all* directions.

Making Educated Guesses

Some children are afraid to guess when they aren't absolutely sure of the answer. Teach your child how to make educated guesses by narrowing down his choices and by playing his hunches. Members of a certain history class once stormed out of the classroom after taking a test. They were furious because the teacher had put questions on the test that were not included on the review sheet. "How are we supposed to remember who the first woman astronaut was," complained one particularly vocal student, "if we weren't told to study that part of the chapter?"

The objectionable question read like this:

Who was the first woman astronaut?
  a. John Glenn
  b. Buzz Aldrin
  c. Sally Ride
  d. Alan Shepard

The teacher included questions like this because 1) the material had been covered in class discussions, and 2) he wanted to show his students how to narrow down their choices and improve their test grades. Students would not have jumped to the conclusion that they couldn't answer the question above if they had read all the possible answers and narrowed them down to the only one that is a female name!

On all but some standardized tests, students are expected to answer all questions. Encourage your child not to leave blank spaces, because unless the teacher specifies differently, guessing cannot lower the test score, but an educated guess might serve to raise it. Some students get into the habit of leaving blank spaces, and others find it easier to claim "I don't know" than to think about the possibilities. To avoid this problem, do not let your child skip parts of his homework assignments; work with him to come up with the best guesses possible. This attitude toward thinking and working through a problem will serve him well at test time.

Although some teachers expect children to give back exact textbook facts on tests, most are delighted by students like Jenny who at least attempt an answer when they aren't sure. Twice last week Jenny found she could not answer test questions from memory, so she let her creative side respond. In answer to the question in social studies "What was the name of George Washington's wife?" Jenny wrote, "Mrs. Washington." When asked on a vocabulary test to define the word "behooves," Jenny wrote, "the feet on bees." Jenny thought about the questions and made an effort to answer. That's one sign of a good test-taker.

Using Time Wisely

Many children stack up one poor test grade on top of the other because they never have time to finish. These grades don't really reflect the children's knowledge, but they are used to indicate pass or fail. You can help your child get over this problem by setting up his homework time as if it were a timed test. Map out a certain amount of work that you believe he should be able to accomplish in a given period of time. Then watch how he progresses through the assignment.

Does your child dillydally or daydream? If he does, point this out to him and let him see the relationship between slow work habits and unfinished papers. To discourage dawdling, try the suggestions on page 119. You might also increase his time-on-task concentration by setting a goal of total uninterrupted work time for 2 minutes. Then when he can work steadily for this amount of time, increase it to 4 minutes. Continue to lengthen the time period until he can concentrate on simple tasks for at least 25 minutes.

If your child has major difficulty concentrating on his work for any extended period of time and you believe his attention deficit is responsible for his poor school grades, talk to his teacher. Your child may need special attention and remedial help that would enable him to take his test in a relaxed environment and in longer time periods with occasional breaks in between sections.

Does your child run out of time because he spends too long on difficult questions? If he does, point this out to him and tell him not to spend so much time on questions that cause him trouble. Tell him to skip over these problem questions then go back to them if time allows at the end.

Reducing Test Anxiety

Some children do poorly on tests because they suffer from a condition called test anxiety. Fear of test-taking can become so intense that it can cause students to avoid studying or to forget everything they did study. Professor Kennedy Hill of the University of Illinois, who has studied test anxiety in children for twenty-five years, says that one-fourth of all elementary-school students are so stressed by tests that they perform substantially below their capabilities. If you think that your child is a "bad test-taker," there are a few things that you can do to relieve his anxiety.

- Help your child become "test smart" by practicing the test-taking tips we've already mentioned and by going over the format of the different kinds of test questions (explained beginning on page 133).
- Boost your child's confidence and decrease his anxiety by assuring him that many people find taking tests a frightening experience.
- Don't belittle your child's fear by insisting that there is nothing to be afraid of. Be positive, uncritical, and patient.
- Offer practice opportunities. Jay Comras, who designed test-preparation material for the National Association of Secondary School Principals, says, "Experienced test-takers score better than inexperienced ones." Ask your child's teacher how tests are given in school. Are they timed? Do they ask mainly for recall of factual information? Or, do they ask for subjective essay-type answers? Ask for old tests that your child can practice with (or make up your own). Then at home, practice under real test-taking conditions. This will help your child learn how to pace himself and will uncover his strengths and weaknesses.

If your child does poorly when tests are timed (as all standardized tests are), help him learn to overcome this fear of being rushed. Time homework assignments, time reading, time laundry-folding and room-cleaning. When he realizes that he is consistently able to finish the work in the time allowed and thus "beat the clock," his anxiety will lessen and his skill at working within the given period will improve.

Types of Tests

Your child will take many different types of tests during his
school years. There are four principal kinds of tests:

1. teacher-made tests,
2. tests that are prepared by commercial publishers and included in text- and workbooks,
3. standardized tests of mental ability (IQ tests), and
4. standardized tests of academic achievement.

In testing terms, *teacher-made* and *workbook tests* are
called "criterion-referenced." They are designed to test students' knowledge of specific instruction; they relate directly
to a child's classwork. Ideally, everyone taking these tests
could score 100 percent. These kinds of tests give you the
best available method of determining how well your child is
learning. This type of test can also be used as a diagnostic
tool to discover where your child needs additional help and
in what areas he is fully competent.

Standardized tests (whether of IQ or academic achievement) are called "norm-referenced." It is statistically prede-
termined that of the students who take these tests, one-half
will score below average and one-half will score above average. Therefore, students are evaluated not by how well they
know the material being tested, but rather by how their
scores compare to others who have also taken the test.
These tests are administered in exactly the same way to
everyone who takes them, every time they are given. Generally, they are administered to large groups of students at
the same time and are machine-scored by an organization
outside the school.[1]

Standardized IQ tests may be given in such a group situation or in a one-on-one situation. These tests do not measure a person's ability to recall factual information, but
rather they evaluate aptitude—that is, the ability to think.
These tests are discussed in detail in Chapter 2.

Standardized achievement tests evaluate a student's knowledge of factual information, and they are given at all levels

of schooling. Many private pre-school and kindergarten programs, for example, base admission on the results of standardized tests. By Georgia law, all public-school children planning to enter the first grade must take a standardized test. Each year, over 4 million elementary and junior-high students take the Iowa Tests of Basic Skills (which some schools use to place students in fast or slow learning tracks). And over 3 million high school students take the Scholastic Aptitude (SAT) or American College Test (ACT) each year as a basis for college admission.

There is great debate among educators about the value of standardized test scores. Some believe they are necessary and effective evaluative tools; others believe they are misleading and too easily influenced by such non-academic factors as test anxiety, cultural bias, and human error (many students have trouble keeping track of the little holes on the answer sheets that must be filled in and correspond properly to the chosen answer). Whatever their value, the scores can be difficult to decipher and are sometimes misleading. Be sure to ask your child's teacher to explain to you *exactly* what the test scores mean and how they are going to be applied to your child's future schooling. The following basic information about standardized test scores will help you better understand the teacher's explanation:

- *Raw score:* Raw scores tell you very little about your child's performance. These scores are simply the sum of correct answers. These numbers are used to convert the test results to the following relative scores.
- *Grade-level score:* These scores indicate what classroom grade level your child seems to have achieved in that particular area of knowledge. For example, a 4.5 grade level equals the expected performance of a child half-way through the fourth grade. Like all averages, it is unlikely that there is a *true* level of performance actually achieved by children on the 4.5 grade level, but these numbers give you an idea of how your child is learning as compared to other children on other grade levels.
- *Percentile score:* These scores rank a child's test score in relation to other students who took the test. If, for example, your child receives a percentile score of 75, this means that 75 percent of the children who took this test (be it a

national, state, or district test) scored lower than your child, and 25 percent scored higher.

Standardized achievement tests are not perfect measures of your child's ability to do well in school; even teacher-made tests have their drawbacks. But the fact is that your child will take these tests and be evaluated by them for the rest of his years in school. You can make the test-taking procedure easier for him by following the suggestions in this chapter and also by viewing tests as a singular and incomplete part of education—not as a do-or-die, all-important, must-achieve situation. Encourage your child to do his best and assure him that the results (good or bad) are only a small part of what he is as a student and as a person.

Test Question Formats

Teacher-made tests, commercial text- and workbook tests, and standardized tests are generally comprised of five types of questions. You can improve your child's ability to do well on these tests by talking with him about the various formats and by suggesting ways to tackle each type of test.

Multiple-choice Tests

On multiple-choice tests, students must select the correct answer from three to five different possible answers. The key to finding the correct one lies in the students' ability to eliminate incorrect answers one by one, thereby narrowing down the choices. Teach your child to find the ones that are absolutely false and cross them off immediately. Then let him practice with homemade or workbook tests, knowing how to think about the remaining answers, and then, using reason and logic, select the correct one.

Sample multiple-choice questions:

1. How many inches are there in a foot?
   a) 4 b) 10 c) 12 d) 20
2. Who discovered the Pacific Ocean?
   a) Columbus b) Balboa c) Valdez d) Ponce de Leon

True-False Tests

On true-false tests, students must decide if a given statement is true or false. These tests make guesswork easy, because a "true" or "false" answer always has a 50 percent chance of being right. Although this makes true or false tests an unreliable measurement of knowledge, they are commonly used.

You can help your child do well on true-false tests by teaching him to look out for qualifying words such as: "all," "always," "no one," "never," "best," or "worst." These words usually make any statement "false." Also, be sure to point out to your child that if a true-false statement has two parts, one of them true and one of them false, the answer is always "false."

Sample true-false questions:
1. All mammals live on land. True   False
2. The sun revolves around the earth; it does this two times a day. True   False

Short-answer Tests

On short-answer tests, students are asked to fill in a blank or correctly complete a statement. These tests rely on the student's ability to recall facts from memory. You can help your child do well on these tests by implementing the memorization techniques explained on page 146. Also, caution him to read the statement carefully; a misread or overlooked word can easily change the meaning of the statement.

Sample short-answer questions:
1. The capital of New York is _____.
2. There are _____ feet in a mile.

Matching Tests

On matching tests, students are asked to take a word or phrase from one column and match it with a term, fact, or idea from a second column. Children do best on matching tests when they:

- Learn to read the directions carefully.
- Read over all the words in both columns before answering any.
- Check to see if the number of items from one column equals the number of items to be matched (this will tell you if you have to use some answers more than once).
- Answer the easy ones first.
- Use the process of elimination and common sense to match the remaining ones.

Sample matching test:
1. noun ＿＿＿ shows action or state of being
2. verb ＿＿＿ a word that describes
3. adjective ＿＿＿ the name of a person, place, or thing

Essay Tests

On essay tests, children are asked to write a collection of sentences to answer a given question. The tests are subjective because students are asked to discuss ideas rather than give pat right or wrong answers, and they are usually given only to upper-grade students who have learned how to write complete sentences in paragraph form.

The best way to handle essay tests is to think about an answer and plan out a format *before* beginning to write. You can help your child prepare for essay questions by practicing the following tips:

- *Read the directions carefully.* Some essay tests give students a choice of questions to answer or specify how long each answer should be.

- *Read over* all *the questions.* Answer the easiest first.
- *Find the key words.* These are words in the question that will give your child a clue as to how the question should be answered. These words include: "list," "explain," "compare," "examine," "describe," and "give the reasons."
- *Stick to the subject and the question.* As you know from conversations with them, kids tend to wander from subject to subject. They will do the same on essay tests unless they're taught how to focus on *one* idea. If the question asks the student to "compare" the causes of the Civil War with the causes of the Revolutionary War, your child will not get extra credit for describing the military uniforms worn in each war.
- *Budget time.* Help your child learn how to answer questions within a given time period. We will be able to do this if he learns to stick to the topic and to say the most in the fewest words. Ideally, he should have enough time to go back and review his answers for mistakes or grammar errors.

Use Old Tests

Tests are used by teachers to measure students' understanding of given information. Their educational value does not end, however, as soon as the test is over. When the test is returned, your child has an opportunity to learn from his mistakes and to gain encouragement and reinforcement from his correct answers. When your child shows you his returned test, do not merely glance at the grade, make a quick comment, and give it back. Use each and every test as a learning opportunity.

Incorrect answers point to areas of information that your child has not mastered. Guide your child in finding the correct answers and make sure he now understands them. This is especially important in subject areas like grammar, math, and science, where one skill is built upon mastery of another.

Graded tests are the ideal tool for practicing test-taking skills. Use them to prepare for future tests. Ask your child to tell you how he answered certain questions, "Did you make an educated guess? Did you eliminate any choices? Did you misread any directions? Were there questions you didn't understand?" By taking the time to review each test, you're helping your child fill in the blanks in his education and also to practice test-taking.

Many decisions about your child's future will be made based on test scores. His academic record will reflect his ability to take tests, and later, scholarships, college acceptance, graduate school programs (in law or medicine, for example), employment opportunities, and promotions all may be given partly on the basis of examination scores. To succeed in our present educational system students must learn how to study and perform well on tests. You can help your child in this key area by giving him the test-taking tips outlined above, and by presenting him with opportunities to practice these skills.

Resource List

Write

- The National PTA
  700 N. Rush Street
  Chicago, Illinois 60611
  Ask for a free copy of the pamphlet "Plain Talk About Tests."
- Consumer Information Center-V
  Box 100
  Pueblo, Colorado 81002
  Send 50 cents for a copy of the booklet "Help Your Child Improve in Test-Taking."

Books

- *The A-Plus Guide to Taking Tests*
  Louise Colligan
  Scholastic Inc., 1984 (grades 7 and up)

7

"But I did study!"

Study Skills that Help Children Learn and Remember

Study Skills

No one is born with study skills in hand. Like all skills, they consist of a number of techniques that must be taught, learned, and practiced. Yet, many school children (even some in first grade!) come home with the vague assignment "Study for your test tomorrow." These children sit down, look at their books, and have no idea what "study" means. This is why many children fail even though they claim, "But I studied!" It is also why parents do study assignments for children who say, "I don't know what to do."

This section will explain a variety of study skills that you should teach to your child so he can then use them to learn and remember his school work by himself. As you teach your child *how* to study, remember the old Chinese proverb that says: "Give a man a fish and you feed him for a day. Teach him *how* to fish and he feeds himself for life." When your child has to study, don't give him a fish, give him what he needs to catch his own.

Get to Know the Textbook

Give your child a guided tour through his textbooks. Most school books are written in structural formats that are geared to enhance the learning process. Unfortunately, in their rush to get through each day's assignments, many students (and teachers) forget to use all the study aids available in the book.

Show your child how to use the table of contents and the index in his books. Read through the table of contents and let your child see where his lessons are taking him and what kind of topics and information he will soon be learning. Also, teach him or remind him how to use the index (an alphabetical subject listing in the back of the book). To illustrate its use, challenge your child to find information about John Henry in the history book, for example, and time how long it takes him with the usual methods of browsing and skimming. Then show him how to find the exact page in the index and try a timed search again with another topic. Index use is a particularly helpful homework tool when your child needs to re-check a fact or fill in a single answer.

Then show your child how to use the glossary. Many students have poured through large dictionaries with multiple-meaning entries trying to define words used in their homework lessons, Then quite by accident they find one day that the words and their definitions as used in the text are right in the back of the book in the glossary. The glossary is an alphabetical listing in the back of the book that defines words *as they are used* in the textbook. This makes it easy for students to relate the definition to their assignment.

Take time to look through the chapter format. Point out how subheads break down the main topic into smaller parts. Note the importance of words in bold or italic print. If the text contains maps, charts, or bar, line, or pie graphs, make sure your child knows how to read them. These are valuable sources of information (and sources of reference information that are always tested on national standardized tests). Most textbooks use these study aids to organize and simplify information, the students have a habit of skipping over them in their reading assignments.

Explain the value of flashback study cues at the end of the chapter. These point out the main ideas and important points in each chapter. Their headings may be something like "In Summary," "Checking Up," "Main Ideas to Think About," "Words to Remember."

Encourage your child to use these helpers to better understand his lesson even if that section is not assigned by the teacher.

Encourage Active Studying

Many homework assignments are completed with an approach called "passive studying." Using this method, a student silently reads a piece of information and hopes to remember the main points. Johnny used this method to do his homework every night. He would read the assigned work and make sure he could answer the questions at the end of each chapter. Johnny's parents knew that he did his work; they knew he tried his best, and so they were confused when his progress report showed that he was having trouble in all of his subjects. Johnny's experience supports research studies that find passive studying to be a most ineffectual method of remembering information. To enhance your child's ability to learn, teach him how to engage in *active studying*.

Active studying requires that a person become involved in the information, give feedback, respond, react, and use as many of the five senses as possible in the learning process. The following are some examples of how children can use active studying.

Oral Reading:

One way to begin active studying is to encourage your child to read aloud—use his voice, hear the sound of the information. Oral reading reduces the mind-wandering that often happens during silent reading. It also helps drown out distractions, such as siblings and TV noises.

Listen to your child's oral readings. When you give him an audience, you also give yourself a chance to tune in to his school lessons and to keep track of his reading abilities. If your schedule won't allow you to give undivided attention to your child's oral reading, have him read to you while you're doing the dishes or folding laundry, etc. Of course, silent reading is sometimes more convenient or even more appropriate (reading silently without sound or lip movement is a skill all children must eventually master), but reading homework assignments aloud occasionally, will serve as an effective study technique.

Talking:

Talking about school assignments is another way to become actively involved in studying. You have probably noticed that you gain a better understanding of a subject if you have a chance to talk about it with your spouse or friends. Talking aloud often gives vague ideas a firmer form, and it can clarify points of confusion. A two-way conversation may also bring up interesting points that you did not originally focus on when you first considered the topic. This same process of thought clarification happens when your child has a chance to talk about his reading assignments.

A typical "talking" study period might sound like this:

Dad: "What are you reading about in your science book?"
David: "Plants."
Dad: "Oh yeah? What about plants?"
David: "Something about photo . . . something."
Dad: "Is it something called 'photosynthesis'?"
David: "Yeah, that's it. How'd you know?"
Dad: "Because I studied that when I was in school too. But I forget exactly what it means. Can you tell me?"
David: "Well, the book said it has something to do with the way plants give us oxygen."
Dad: "How do they do that?"
David: "It happens in two steps. First plants take in sunlight and carbon something-or-other."
Dad: "Dioxide—carbon dioxide."
David: "Yeah, carbon dioxide. Then the plant changes them into food for itself and oxygen for us."

As you can see from this conversation, David's dad is helping him better understand this reading assignment without making David feel like he's being quizzed or challenged. David had read the assignment; he had answered the questions at the end (which kids can do easily without having the slightest idea what the material is really all about), and so he considered the subject closed. It was not until he tried to explain it back to his dad that he really came to understand it. Even the simple act of saying out loud a new vocabulary word like "photosynthesis" helps to reinforce the lesson.

Writing:

The act of writing something down supports the learning process. Writing makes a child go over important points one word at a time. It involves active physical movement and brings one more of the child's senses (that of touch) into play.

In the "old days," students would copy complete chapter outlines off the blackboard; they would take daily notes from their teacher's lectures and go home and copy information from the textbook into their notebooks. Although these writing assignments are still often practiced, photo copies, dittos, and fill-in-the-blank workbooks often take the place of writing. Although work is now done more quickly and efficiently, students have lost opportunities to reinforce their grasp of the facts through writing.

As your child reads through his assignments, encourage him to write down the important points. (Older children can make actual outlines.) At first he will complain, "I don't have to do that!" But persist in your request, help him, and praise him for any effort he makes to write down facts he wants to remember.

Role Playing:

Give your child a break from the routine of always taking *in* information. Reinforce his lessons by letting him give *out* information by taking on the role of the teacher.

Young children will enjoy "teaching" their stuffed animals, dolls, friends, and younger siblings. It is especially fun if you help your child set up a "classroom" with a chalkboard, and teacher and student chairs. This role-playing allows the young student to organize newly learned information and give it back in some kind of understandable form.

Older children may laugh at such a dramatic idea. Don't let that stop you from pushing the technique. Encourage your child to pretend he is the teacher and you are a pupil who doesn't understand the lesson. Ask him to explain it to you in a very simple way so you can pass a test on the material. In this role of the teacher, your child can also pull more out of his study time if he makes up a test on the material he is studying. This pushes him to look through the information, find important facts and concepts, write them down in question form, and, of course as the teacher, know the answers.

Demonstrating:

Learning becomes more game-like (and therefore easier) when you and your child work together to find ways to demonstrate the facts of a lesson. Try the following whenever appropriate and use your imagination to find other ways to turn abstract concepts into concrete examples.

- *Use everyday, sitting-around-the-house objects to give meaning to otherwise dull information.* You might, for example, pep up a vocabulary lesson (and at the same time make the words easier to remember) by using a tower made of building blocks to demonstrate the meaning of the word "demolish." Or if, for example, your child is studying George Washington's trip across the Delaware River, take some action figure toys, put them in a toy boat, and sail them across your kitchen sink while your child tells you what's happening to George and his men.
- *Give your child the real thing.* If he's studying plants, give him a plant to examine; if he's learning how to tell time, take your clock off the wall and give it to him; if he's learning how to add coin money, give him pennies, nickels, dimes, and quarters to count.
- *Give your child clay, paint, crayons, and the like.* Ask him to create a model or a picture of what he's studying. Ask him to draw a picture of a Viking in battle, or to paint the sunrise on the horizon as Columbus might have seen it from his ship, or to build an Eskimo igloo from sugar cubes

• or white clay. These projects shouldn't be "assigned" as additional work; make them a playtime activity that is labeled "fun."

Whenever possible, let your child use all his senses when he's learning new things. Let him touch, smell, hear, taste, as well as see his assignments. You can do this by encouraging your child to use and combine the active study methods of oral reading, talking, writing, role playing, and demonstrating. The chart below compares the learning steps of passive and active studying. Which method of studying do you think will be most effective in helping him to learn the facts?

Passive Study	*Active Study*
• read silently • re-read silently	• read aloud • talk about what you've read • write down the main points • teach the information to a friend • draw a picture about the topic

Read for Understanding

There will be times during the course of your child's education when it will not be possible or appropriate to use all the active studying techniques we've described. There are many assignments that must be done quietly and in solitude. These kinds of lessons often involve reading through a given chapter and answering the questions to test comprehension at the end. It is generally believed that if a child can answer the questions, he understands the material. Unfortunately, that is not true at all.

Nine-year-old Colleen's parents and teacher think she is lazy. They insist that she can do her assignments if she would just concentrate. They believe that she isn't trying her best when she stumbles through oral readings and when she slams down her books and cries, "I can't do it!" Her parents "know" she can do better because her test scores in reading comprehension are always very high. "You can read this lesson, if you just try," her parents and teacher insist. Colleen herself doesn't understand why she can answer questions about passages she can't really read, but she does know she's trying her best and still getting low grades.

See for yourself how easily a child can fall into this predicament. Read the following passage and then answer the "comprehension" questions that follow.

Corandic is an emurient grof with many fribs; it granks from corite, an olg which cargs like lange. Corite grinkles several other tarances, which garkers excarp by glarcking the corite and starping it in tranker-clarped storbs.

1. What is corandic?
2. What does corandic grank from?
3. How do garkers excarp the tarances from the corite?[1]

If you were able to answer these questions, people might assume you know all about corandics and you are ready to move on to the next level of information that is built on this foundation of facts. See how easily a child could get lost? One way to improve reading comprehension is with the SQ3R technique that follows.

SQ3R:

You can help your child learn how to read assignments for meaning and understanding by teaching him a technique called SQ3R for "Survey," "Question," "Read," "Recite," "Review". This method was developed by Dr. Frank Robinson in 1946[2] and has been found over the years to be an effective learning tool because it incorporates several methods of learning into one strategy. In the beginning you and your child may feel that this method drags out homework assignments, but with practice you'll both soon see that it actually makes work easier to do and remember. Explain the method to your child in this way:

Step 1: Survey

To begin, take a few minutes to look over the material to be studied. Knowing a little about a topic makes it easier to read with understanding. Read the title and bold print subheadings, and read the introductory and summary paragraphs. Be sure also to look at all the pictures, graphs, and charts.

Step 2: Question

As you survey the material, ask yourself questions that you think will be answered in the text. For example, if a bold subhead reads, "Pilgrims Land at Plymouth Rock," ask yourself, "Where's Plymouth Rock?" "When did the pilgrims land there?" "What did they find there?" Or, if the subhead reads, "The Metric System," turn that heading into a question like, "What is the metric system?" Be sure to read over the questions at the end of the material. They offer a good preview of the important points that will be explained in the reading.

Step 3: Read

With the background information and insight gathered in Steps 1 and 2, read the assignment. You'll find that as you read your thoughts are more organized and you can answer the questions you thought of in Step 2.

Step 4: Recite

This step asks you to engage in active study techniques to help you remember what you read. Talk about the material, write down notes and the answers to your questions from Step 2, and then read them aloud.

Step 5: Review

To increase your ability to recall the information from the assignment, go back over what you've read and read over your notes. You should do this at the end of the study period and then again one or two times during the following week.

Help your children get into the habit of reviewing. Encourage them to read over their notes during what otherwise would be wasted time (like the time spent waiting for the school bus, waiting for siblings to get out of the bathroom, waiting for breakfast or dinner, etc.) Every time they read over a few facts, increases the brain's ability to remember.

Teach Memorization Skills

Children need to learn how to memorize because there are times when memorization is the most practical and effective study tool. It is especially appropriate when learning things such as multiplication tables, names of famous people, dates in history, laws in science, spelling rules, and the like. The following methods will help teach your child *how* to learn through memorization.

Repetition:

The most commonly used method of memorizing is through repetition. Remember when you would take a fact out of the text and say it over and over and over again, hoping to make it stick in your brain? "Columbus discovered America in 1492. Columbus discovered America in 1492. Columbus discovered America in 1492." You may have remembered this fact for the test the next day, but the method you used was quite difficult, boring, and sometimes ineffective. Repetition *will* help your child to remember things, but if it is the only method of memorization he uses, he won't remember correctly or for long. Children who try to memorize the Lord's Prayer through repetition alone, for example, often inadvertently illustrate the problems with this kind of rote learning when they pray with zeal: ". . . and lead us not into Penn Station." In the same way, the pledge to the flag can become a pledge "to the United States of America and to the Republic of Richard Sands." Obviously, rote repetition is not intended to promote understanding.

Repetition used alone may also fall short of its goal because it often brings information only into the short-term memory bank—a place in the brain where facts and ideas are stored for short periods of time. You use your short-term memory, for example, when you look up a phone number in the directory and say it over and over again while you grab the phone and dial. The number will stay in mind for this short period. But if you get a busy signal and have to dial again a few minutes later, you will probably have to look up the number once again because it's no longer in your memory bank.

Kids will often try to stuff information into their short-term memory and hope it will stay there just long enough to get them through the test. After the test is over their recall of the information is nil. In this way, they pass the test but have learned nothing. Because this happens so easily and so often, it is important to teach your child how to store memorized information in his long-term memory bank. He can best do this by learning how to use repetition along with other such memory devices as association, finding parts of the whole, rhyming, and using flash cards to support his lessons.

Association:

New information stays in our long-term memory best when it can attach itself to knowledge we already have. The process by which this happens is called association. If, for example, the last four digits of the phone number that you look up in the directory are the same as the four numbers of your birthdate, you won't have to look up that number again because you can attach it to a number you have already memorized.

Your child can learn to use association to improve his memory in many different ways. If, for example, he must memorize the names of the first five presidents of the United States, he can look at them in order and then try to find some way to recall them easily.

First he should make a list:

1. Washington
2. Adams
3. Jefferson
4. Madison
5. Monroe

Rather than sitting for 20 minutes saying the names over and over again, he might associate the first letters of the names with the nonsense word: WAJ-MA-MO. The next day in school this silly word will help him recall the information he needs:

W A J MA MO

Washington, Adams, Jefferson, Madison, Monroe.

Or, he might create a sentence in which the first letter of each word will match the first letter of each president's name:

Willy And Jim Made Models.

Washington Adams Jefferson Madison Monroe

He might even remember the reverse order of the presidents' names by imagining someone's exclamation upon seeing a shark:

"Ma! Mo! Jaw!"

Ma = Madison, Mo = Monroe, J = Jefferson, A = Adams, W = Washington

This may seem like a ridiculous way to study, but it works; in fact, the sillier the association, the better it works!

You may have already used this kind of word association without knowing it. In music it is used to label the spaces of the treble staff, which are f,a,c,e; they spell the word "face." The lines of this staff are e,g,b,d,f and are often remembered with the sentence "Every good boy deserves fudge." The technique is also used by many students to remember the first letters of the global directions, which spell the word "news" (N = north, E = east, W = west, S = south), and the first letters of the Great Lakes, which create the acronym "homes" (H = Huron, O = Ontario, M = Michigan, E = Erie, S = Superior). When your child has a list to memorize, encourage him to isolate the initial letters and then associate them with a real or nonsense word or make a sentence out of them.

Parts of the Whole:

You can also improve your child's ability to memorize information by urging him to look inside large pieces of information to find smaller pieces that he can more easily remember. This works especially well with spelling and vocabulary lessons.

Ten-year-old Jamie found this method to be the answer to his spelling problem. He had misspelled two words on his last spelling test. His teacher told him to write those words correctly ten times each and then she re-tested him. Again he spelled them incorrectly. At home that night, Jamie complained to his mother that he just could not remember whether to spell the first problem word, "Separate" or "seperate." His mom looked closely at the word, then she pulled out a clue to help Jamie remember the correct spelling. "Always remember," she said, "the word 'separate' has a rat in it." "Yeah, I see it!" laughed Jamie.

The second problem word was "villain." This gave Jamie trouble because it has an unexpected silent "a" in it. Again Jamie's mother looked closely at the word. "Okay, Jamie," she said, "I think this sentence will help you remember how to spell that word: 'A villain lives in a villa in town.' Do you see how the two words 'villa in' spell out your problem word?" "Yeah. thanks, Mom," Jamie said. "I'm gonna tell my teacher that I know how to spell those words without even writing them over a hundred times like she suggested." Next week, Jamie's mom will begin to help Jamie find his own memory clues in difficult words.

Vocabulary lessons are also easier to remember if your child can find a piece of a word that he already knows within the larger word. The word "malodorous," for example, is difficult to remember on its own, but if your child notices the smaller word "odor" (which is a word that he knows) inside the difficult word, his task of memorizing will be made easier.

Association is often built on clues that must be pulled out of the material to be memorized. Your child may have to search for these memory hooks, but that's the fun of studying with association and it's also a part of the memorization process. Looking at the information, taking it apart, and finding meaningful ways to put it back together will itself help your child to learn and remember.

Rhyming:

Facts are more easily remembered when they are placed in a rhyme. You've used this memorization device yourself if any of these rhymes sound familiar to you:

"Thirty days hath September, April, June, and November . . ."
"I before e except after c . . .'"
"In 1492 Columbus sailed the ocean blue."

Look how easily facts of multiplication can be memorized when they are rhymed in this *School House Rock*[3] song:

You multiply 7 × 1; I got 7 days to get the job done.
You multiply 7 × 2; take 14 laughs when you're feeling blue.
You multiply 7 × 3; a 21-day vacation to play with me.
You multiply 7 × 4; ya got 28 days, that's one month more, to pay the mortgage on your store.
You multiply 7 × 5; I don't know how you did it but man alive, that's 35!

If you or your child has a flair for poetry, take the challenge and rhyme those hard-to-remember facts.

Flashcards:

No chapter on study skills would be complete without mention of flashcards. Flashcards are used to teach facts through visual repetition. Many parents like the ease of flashcard study, and some use them with their children from infancy through junior high school. These cards are helpful any time a large number of facts need to be learned. They can be used for such things as definitions, dates, names and facts about people, formulas, and new words. The International Reading Association suggests that if your child uses flashcards, you try these ideas:

• When using cards for the first time, put them into small groups. Learn one group of cards at a time.

- Shuffle the cards often so they aren't learned in a particular order.
- Practice often for short periods of time.
- Spend most of the time on cards that haven't been mastered yet.[4]

When using flashcards, keep in mind that repetition alone is a weak method of learning anything. Flashcards are a most effective study aid when used in combination with other methods. You might, for example, put sight words on flashcards to support a phonics lesson. Or, you could use homemade flash cards as part of Step 5 in the SQ3R method to review studied material. Or, you could encourage your child to make flash cards himself; this would engage him in the act of writing down his lesson and also give him a source of review material. Flashcards will probably always have a place in the educational process, so use them *with* other methods of study and they can help your child to learn.

Study skills are tools your children will need for the rest of their lives. The ability to organize, think, read, understand, and remember is the cornerstone of all intellectual achievement. Yet unfortunately they are skills that are not generally included in the classroom curriculum. The next time your child sits down to study, work with him to build study habits that include active studying, the SQ3R reading method, and a variety of the memorization techniques explained in this chapter.

Resource List

Write

- International Reading Association
  800 Barksdale Road
  PO Box 8139
  Newark, Delaware 19714
  Ask for a free copy of the pamphlet "Studying: A Key to Success . . . Ways Parents Can Help."

Books

- *Every Kid's Guide to Thinking and Learning*
  Joy Berry
  Childrens, 1987 (for grades 3 to 7)
- *Help Your Son or Daughter Study for Success*
  Dan Vogler and David Hutchins
  M. Damien Publishers, 1985
- *Learning to Learn*
  Carl Haag
  Harcourt Brace Jovanovich, 1961

Computer Software

- *Magic Spells*
  The Learning Company (1-800-852-2255)
  Ages: 6 to 12
  Apple II Series, IBM/Tandy and compatibles
  This program builds essential spelling skills.
- *Grammar Gremlins*
  Davidson Associates, Inc. (1-800-556-6141)
  Ages: 9 to 12
  Apple; IBM PC, PC Jr. and PS/2; Tandy 1000 series; major compatibles
  This program includes more than 60 rules and 600 practice sentences in four levels of difficulty.
- *Early Education I*
  KIDware (catalog #67048)
  Ages: 3 to 7
  Commodore 64 or 128
  The program contains numbers, letters, counting exercises, and early math.
- *Library Search and Solve*
  K-12 Micromedia Publishing
  Grade levels: 4th to 8th grade
  Apple
  This program will encourage your child to learn and practice library research skills.

8

"Your teacher said *what!?*"

A Look at the Parent/Child/Teacher Relationship

"My teacher is mean to me," complained 9-year-old Danny. "Every day she yells at me, and I don't do anything wrong. Today she gave me a bad grade just because she doesn"t like me. You gotta get me out of her class!" Danny's parents know that kids tend to exaggerate the monster-like qualities of their teachers. They have assured Danny that if he behaves and does his work, his teacher will have no reason to pick on him. "But you gotta believe me," insisted Danny. "Tonight's back-to-school night; go and tell her to leave me alone, please!" "We can't, Danny," said his mom. "Dad has a project due tomorrow that he has to work on tonight, and I promised Grandma I'd take her to the church meeting. You go do your homework and settle down in that class. I'm sure everything will be fine."

Creating a Positive Parent/Child/Teacher Relationship

Danny's parents have always stayed involved in his school work. They monitor his homework, insist on quality work and good attendance, limit the time he can watch TV or play video games, and make sure he is well-fed and -rested. This time, however, they're missing their chance to involve Danny's teacher in their efforts to give Danny academic support. Whether Danny is right or wrong about his teacher's attitude, his negative feelings will interfere with his ability to reach his potential in this class, and so his parents should investigate the problem.

This doesn't mean that Danny's parents should have taken him at his word, raced over to the school, stormed into the classroom, and confronted the teacher with angry accusations. This too would have been a mistake because quality education grows out of the positive and cooperative efforts of the parents, child, and teacher. The best way to build a positive relationship with your child's teacher is to avoid conflicts right from the start. The following sections will tell you how to do this at home, at back-to-school nights, and at parent/teacher conferences. Then the chapter will explain what to do if a conflict does arise.

At Home

Children learn best from people they respect. That's why you should always speak about your child's teacher with respect and insist that your child follow your example. You can set the stage for a respectful and positive attitude toward a teacher before your child has a chance to think otherwise. As soon as you learn who your child's teacher will be, say something nice about him or her (no matter how you really feel). Remember that teachers' reputations are often based on hearsay or individual conflicts that occurred in the past. Never repeat the neighborhood stories about "bad" teachers to your child, and don't let him bend your ear about the awful things so-and-so said about this person. Just as teachers should welcome each child into the classroom without holding grudges about what they've heard happened last year, so should your child give his new teacher a fair chance. If you later find that the teacher really *is* unbearable, then it's time for action as explained later in this chapter. But in the majority of cases, stories about "nasty" teachers are just rumors and shouldn't be allowed to influence the way your child approaches his schooling.

Support the teacher's goals and assignments. If your child comes home with an assignment that looks to you to be a waste of time or too laborious to serve any constructive purpose, talk about it with the teacher—not your child. Children can't learn to respect teachers or the educational process itself if you encourage negative feelings by saying things like, "That's the dumbest thing I ever heard of!"

You can also foster a good parent/child/teacher relationship by doing what you can to motivate the teacher. Too many parents contact the school only when something goes wrong. Show your child's teacher that you appreciate his or her efforts by making a quick phone call or writing a note that says something like, "My daughter was thrilled to be chosen for a part in last week's class play." Or, "Thank you for inviting my son to bring his pet to school. He's never been this excited about a class assignment." You might even write a note to the school principal to acknowledge and praise an especially good lesson or opportunity your child was given by his teacher. Give your child's teacher some positive attention and you'll probably find that he or she will give the same back to your child.

At Back-to-School Night

In the beginning of the school year, most schools across the country invite parents to a back-to-school night. This is an opportunity for you to visit your child's classroom, to enjoy the artwork and class papers hung on the bulletin boards, and to sit in your child's seat and listen to his teacher explain the goals and curriculum of that grade level. This is the perfect setting in which to gain some insight into the teacher's personality, attitudes, and teaching methods. It is also an opportunity to show your child that you're interested in his school work and that you value education.

This is *not* a good time to initiate a personal conversation about your individual child. Although many parents try to engage the teacher in long intimate discussions, this is inappropriate and rude because it robs other parents of the opportunity to use this time for what it is intended—a chance to simply introduce themselves. Make sure to say hello and add something positive. (It has been found that teachers often look with favor on students whose parents show they are interested in and supportive of the educational system.)

If you have specific concerns to talk about, slip the teacher a note with your phone number and ask him or her to call you so you can set up a convenient time to talk about your child.

At Parent/Teacher Conferences

Some schools schedule parent/teacher conferences on a regular basis for every parent, regardless of how the child is doing in school. Other schools arrange these meetings only on a when-called-for basis. In either case, these conferences are often faced with mixed feelings by both the parents and teachers. Ideally conferences are the perfect opportunity to develop a partnership that helps children do their best in school. But too often, unfortunately, they become awkward confrontations in which both sides leave the room no more enlightened or motivated than when they entered.

You can get the most out of your parent/teacher conferences by following this list of Do's and Don't's.

DO:

- Talk to your child before the conference. Find out what he likes and dislikes about his teacher and class work. Ask him if he wants you to talk to the teacher about anything specific.
- Jot down a list of questions that you want to ask the teacher. Keep in mind that time is usually short; limit your questions to those that will give you the information you need to help your child perform to his best ability. Some questions suggested by the National PTA include:

  Is my child working up to ability?
  Is he unusually shy or aggressive?
  Are there any special behavior or learning problems that I should be aware of?
  Is my child's homework finished when it is turned in?

What can I do at home to enhance the classroom lessons?

- Tell the teacher about any situations at home (such as divorce, death, birth, or a move) that may be affecting your child's performance.
- Listen to the teacher's side of a story without interrupting. Very often Johnny-at-home is not the same child as Johnny-at-school. Let the teacher fill you in on the other side of your child's personality.
- Focus on solving problems, not placing blame. Approach solutions with an attitude that says, "What can *we* do to help my child?"
- Ask for an explanation if the teacher says something you don't understand.
- End the conference by summing up decisions you've made together.

DON'T:

- Cancel a conference because you have to work, or you are ill, or for any other reason. *Reschedule* to a time that is convenient for both of you. If that's impossible, be sure to at least arrange a phone conference.
- Become angry or aggressive when you disagree with a teacher. Stay calm and listen. Then present your view of the story and look for some common ground (such as "We both want Cindy to do well in school") from which to work.
- Jump to conclusions before you've investigated. If your child says, "My teacher says you feed me terrible food," don't sit and fume over it or go to a conference ready for battle. A phone call or a visit with the teacher may tell you that because your child is learning about the four main food groups, he concluded (without prompting from his teacher) that he is not eating properly.
- Make promises that you may not be able to keep. It may seem appropriate at the conference to promise, "I will have Jimmy read aloud to me every night for 15 minutes." But if your schedule won't allow you to follow through, it's better to be honest and say, "Most

nights there just isn't time after the homework is done and the kids are bathed and fed for me to give Jimmy extra help time. Is there an after-school tutor program in this town? Is there something my older daughter can help him with? Is there any time during the day when you could individualize some of his work?" If you and the teacher agree to work together, Jimmy will get the attention he needs without anyone making empty promises.

- Hesitate to act if you believe that the teacher is hurting your child educationally or emotionally. The following section will discuss what you can do when your child and his teacher seem to be genuinely mismatched.

Resolving a Teacher/Child Conflict

Even when you make an honest effort to build a positive working relationship with your child's teacher you may someday find yourself faced with a conflict. If you have reason to doubt a teacher's judgment, or if you believe that your child isn't learning as he should, it's best to approach the teacher first with your concerns. Calmly present the problem from your point of view. (Don't try to place blame or convince the teacher he or she is incompetent.) And suggest that the two of you work together to find a cause for the problem and an acceptable solution.

For example, if a child had been absent, careless, or confused at crucial points of instruction, he may be lacking fundamental skills. This will not only cause his grades to fall, but can also cause him to act out his frustration by blaming the teacher and/or by being disruptive in class. Look into this possibility with his teacher. Review your child's classwork and attendance record, and ask the teacher if he or she can pin-point a specific area of weakness. If your child needs remedial or supplemental help, find out how he can get it.

You should also talk to the teacher about the style of

organization and discipline that is practiced in the class-room. If it is very different from yours at home, your child may be having trouble adjusting to the change of expecta-tions and come away feeling, "My teacher picks on me." Knowing this, you can help your child adapt to the situation by explaining that home and school sometimes operate with different sets of rules. You can then ease the confusion by trying to make the two match as much as possible.

Some children claim that school is a waste of time because the teacher is boring and doesn't teach anything new. When this happens it may be because the classwork isn't challeng-ing enough for the child. If, for example, your child is doing multiplication tables at home while the class is learning addition, he may become very frustrated. if you feel that this is the case, ask the teacher to give your child some advanced independent work to do while the others are going over the basics. It's quite obvious how sometimes in the daily grind of working with twenty to thirty students a teacher may overlook your child's special needs. But if you call attention to them, most educators will be willing to acknowledge and consider them when making assignments.

If, after you've voiced your complaints or concerns, you cannot get results or cooperation from the teacher, then you may have to present your case to the principal. Keep in mind, however, that if you do this you may make the teacher feel uneasy and this could certainly affect his or her relationship with your child. Try to minimize any hard feel-ings by telling the teacher that you plan to do this, invite him or her to attend the conference, and suggest that the purpose is to involve an objective third party who may be able to find a mutually acceptable solution to the problem.

When you meet with the principal, come prepared. Docu-ment your concerns, affirm your interest to work with the teacher, and plan to stay calm and avoid placing blame. You might ask the principal to arrange for an impartial observa-tion of the teacher in action. In this way you may find out if your child really is a troublemaker, or if the teacher really is disorganized, or if your child's view of the problem is accu-rate. With this information in hand, you, the teacher, and the principal can more readily come to agreement about a plan of action.

Another option is to ask for a chance to sit in on the classroom yourself. Of course, your child will be on his best behavior for you, but you'll still gain considerable insight into the kind of teaching methods and classroom management methods that are being used by the teacher. When you visit, bring the checklist that follows. The more often you can check off characteristics, the more likely it is that the teacher is not the problem.

CHARACTERISTICS OF A GOOD TEACHER

- The teacher seems to know each child's needs. He or she relates classwork to the children's interests, talents, and hobbies.
- The teacher regularly assigns homework that has an obvious purpose.
- The teacher sets high standards and encourages all students to meet them.
- The teacher creates a warm, friendly, and caring atmosphere that tells the children he or she wants to be there with them.
- The teacher treats all children fairly and does not play favorites.
- The teacher uses a positive code of discipline that is based on clear, fair rules and that reinforces positive behavior more than it punishes negative behavior.
- The teacher varies the teaching methods to make learning fun.

If, after your own observation of your child's teacher, you decide that person is not a good teacher for your child, then it's time to re-think your original plan to work out an acceptable solution with the teacher. Now you have two new choices: grin and bear or have your child put into a different class.

Grin and Bear

The fact is that some teachers are better than others, and it's very unlikely that your child will consistently have only the best. Some years you will disagree with a teacher's style of teaching; other times you may feel that there is a personality conflict between the teacher and your child (as explained in Chapter 2). Or, you may find the teacher to be bossy, boring, or burnt-out. When this happens—and it may well—your child's interests will often be best served if you simply acknowledge that yes, this is not an ideal situation but that's how life is sometimes. Because life is not always made to order, children need to learn how to function in less than perfect circumstances. They need to develop a positive mental attitude in the face of difficulty, and they benefit from learning to interact with different personality types. Children need opportunities like this to learn real-life coping skills.

You can help your child learn to cope by focusing his attention on effort and on the classwork, rather than on the teacher. (Chapter 9 will give you practical and easy ways to do this.) While no one likes to see a child penalized because of the personality characteristics of adults, these circumstances, when unavoidable, do help them prepare to handle the trying times of life.

Remove Your Child

There may come a time when you believe that your young child needs nurturing educational experiences more than coping experiences. In cases of extreme disagreement, you might request that your child be transferred to a different teacher. This is a more practical plan of action than trying to have the teacher removed. (Unless there is concrete evidence of mental instability, drug addiction, or moral depravity, it is very difficult to have a teacher fired.)

Talk to the principal about your wishes to change teachers and do not let yourself get caught in a situation in which the administrators tell you in September that it's too early to make that decision, and then they say in January that it's too late to switch teachers. Once you've tried all other options and have then made up your mind to take the child out of the class, the change is appropriate at any time. You have a right to insist on the change or to go to the superintendent or board of education to present your case.

If you still are not satisfied with the response, you can enroll your child in a different school as a last resort. If you are taking your child from a public school to a private one, this option is usually an expensive one; so think this move over very carefully. It could easily happen that after you change your child's school, friends, and environment, he might find himself stuck with an awful teacher once again!

Whatever options you choose to pursue, remember that throughout the negotiations with school officials, you should refrain from talking openly against the teacher or the school in front of your child. Children commonly transfer the negative comments you make about the teacher to education in general.

Be Involved

You can further enhance the parent/child/teacher relationship by finding ways to become involved in your child's school. Take a good look at your schedule, interests, and abilities and, if possible, volunteer some of your time to the school. You might do this by attending school-sponsored activities such as sports events, theatrical shows, or carnivals. You might also offer to supervise field trips to give your time as a teacher's aide or library assistant, or to organize fund-raisers.

Like 6.6 million other people, you might become involved in your child's education by joining the PTA. This is a national, volunteer association that seeks to unite the home, school, and community in promoting the education, health, and safety of children, youth, and families. At PTA meetings you can keep an open dialogue between yourself, the teachers, and the school administrators. This is an opportunity for involvement that we as parents should make every effort to take advantage of.

Resource List

Write

- National PTA Headquarters
  700 N. Rush Street
  Chicago, Illinois 60611
  Ask for the free PTA publication "Making Parent-Teacher Conferences Work for Your Child." You might also want to subscribe to the National PTA's award-winning magazine, *PTA Today*, which is published seven times a year. This magazine focuses on topics of concern to parents, educators and those interested in the well-being of children. Send $7.00 for a one-year subscription.

Books

- *The National PTA Talks to Parents: How to Get the Best Education for Your Child*
  Melitta J. Cutright
  Doubleday, 1989

9

"Why is school stuff always so boring?"

Individualizing Reading, Writing, Math, and Science Lessons

One night while doing homework, 10-year-old Kyle slammed down his pen and declared, "This is boring. Who cares about amphibians?" "Yeah," chimed in his 7-year-old brother, Keith. "Reading this school book is dumb too. I want to play with my baseball cards."

Keith and Kyle are right; sometimes school work is dry and boring. But when their mom overheard this conversation, she knew that what Keith and Kyle needed was a broader and more personalized look at their school lessons. The next day she took Kyle to a pet store and bought him two small turtles, a large fish bowl, and a supply of turtle food. Suddenly, to Kyle, amphibians were the most fascinating creatures on earth. Later that night she handed Keith a copy of *Baseball Digest*. "I hear there are some good stories in this magazine," she said. "Want to read one with me?" Suddenly, to Keith, reading wasn't so dumb.

This chapter will help you learn to use your child's interests and home activities to enhance his classroom lessons. Through suggested activities, games, and projects, it will teach you how to personalize and vitalize the aspects of reading, writing, math, and science that might seem dull in a textbook, but are really an integral and fascinating part of our everyday lives.

Reading

The International Reading Association says, "The truly literate are not those who know how to read, but those who read—fluently, responsively, critically, and because they want to."[1] We agree. To help your child be one of the truly literate, put away your at-home workbooks and skill sheets; leave phonics and comprehension tests to the teachers. At home, you can create the most effective reading program ever devised simply by finding ways to show your child that reading is fun.

Children who find reading pleasurable will, naturally, read more often. This alone will make your child a better reader. This is proven by research, which has found that children who spend less than five minutes a day reading books receive average scores on standardized reading tests. On the other hand, children who score in the 90th percentile on standardized tests spend at least 20 minutes reading each day. In fact, many educators believe that the amount of time a child spends reading at home is the best predictor of academic growth. What better reason can there be to help your child grow into the reading habit?

Model Good Reading Habits

You can't encourage your child to read by making reading a daily chore, a mechanical activity. But you can encourage your child every day of your life by showing that *you* enjoy reading. Let him see you reading. Comment aloud about interesting facts you uncover. Show the value of reading directions, recipes, and how-to material. Share the pleasure of relaxing with a magazine or novel. It is well known that children imitate their parents—the good and the bad. Use this fact to model a love of reading, and then give your child time and encouragement to follow your lead.

Tap into Your Child's Interests and Needs

You can also directly lead your child to uncover the pleasure of reading. Although it's best not to try to "teach" your child how to read, you can use at-home reading to complement school work. If, for example, your child is studying the colonization of America, ask your librarian to recommend a fiction book that is set in America during the time period of the 1600s. Or, if your child shows an interest in a specific science lesson, give him books that will supplement his text and expand his knowledge. Or, when your child is having trouble grasping a particular geography lesson, lead him to other books that might present the facts in a more interesting format.

Even reluctant readers have personal interests and hobbies that can be used to create reading opportunities. If, for example, your child wants a gerbil, first help him find a book that explains how to properly care for this pet. Or, if he is going on vacation to an unfamiliar place, get him brochures, maps, and books about this place. Or, if your child joins a sports team, bring him to the library so he can select a book that explains the rules, or gives a historical account of the sport, or presents a biography of a famous player. If you tell your child that he needs sharpened reading skills to do well in life, he won't be inspired to read. But if you tell him that a book can explain how to build his much-desired backyard treehouse, he'll be hooked.

Read Aloud

It is a well-documented fact that parents can build reading skills by reading aloud to their young children. But did you know that you can continue this practice with positive results long after your child learns to read for himself? Few school-age children are able to read at a level as high as their understanding, yet unfortunately, after the age of 7 or 8, they are left alone to read only those stories they are able to read to themselves. Don't forsake reading aloud as your child gets older. Besides imparting the pure joy of sharing stories, reading aloud to school-age children has express benefits: it will expand their vocabularies as they hear new words used in context; it will enrich their base of general knowledge by allowing them to explore places and things they can't explore in person and can't read about for themselves; and it will strengthen your parent/child relationship because children are never too "big" to need the physical closeness that read-aloud time gives them.

When you read aloud to your child you can inconspicuously increase his reading skills by asking a few well-placed questions. Questioning during reading can help your child learn to make predictions and comparisons, to analyze characterization, and to comprehend plot development (without ever using any of these literary terms!). Avoid questions that sound like a test of the facts or ask for simple "Yes" or "No" responses. Try questions like:

- What do you think will happen next?
- Did it end as you expected?
- Do you know any other stories that are like this one?
- What did the character in the story learn?
- How is the story character like you?
- How is the family like or different from ours?
- Does the main character seem like a real person?

Answering these questions will encourage your child to talk about the story or piece of information. This communication adds yet another dimension to the learning-through-reading experience.

Unplug the TV

Most parents know the value of building a strong foundation in reading skills, and they certainly would like to do this for their children, but they often say, "there just isn't enough time in the day to sit down and read a story." It's true that we all live in a busy, fast-paced world that sometimes robs us of family leisure time. However, if you re-evaluate your family's TV-viewing habits, you might find that the TV is the real time-robber.

Television watching affects children's reading abilities in two ways. First, too much watching leads to the habit of passive reception of rapidly changing input, which makes children impatient with the active mental effort that is required by reading. And second, TV viewing fills up the time that could otherwise be used to practice and enjoy reading. The next time you're about to say, "Turn on the TV and let's see what's on," stop and say, "let's see what this book (magazine or newspaper) is all about."

Literature or Comics?

The resource list at the end of this chapter will tell you how to find quality pieces of literature to share with your children. Picture books, read-alouds, poetry, fiction, and non-fiction are all excellent ways to expose children to the vast range of human emotion and experiences that are captured in books. However, you can't force-feed quality. If your children will read only comic books or teen-idol magazines—so be it for now. At least they're reading. But don't ever give up the daily reading schedule or your efforts to lead them down other avenues of prose and poetry that in time they too may come to enjoy.

Reading is a fundamental skill that affects a child's ability to do well in all school subjects and ultimately in life. Knowing this, many school districts continually buy expensive new reading programs; President Bush has designated a National Year of the Reader, and Congress has declared war on illiteracy. However, despite these positive measures, our children will not become fully literate unless they believe that reading is important and fun. They will not be convinced unless those who love and care for them show through their own actions that reading is a valued, pleasurable everyday activity. As a parent of a school-age child, the bulk of this responsibility falls to you. Leave the reading lessons and drills in the classroom and journey with your child into the adventurous, humorous, emotional, and factual realm of reading.

Writing

Learning to write is like learning to play a musical instrument. Both are skills that need to be practiced. The only way to learn how to play the piano is to *play*; the only way to learn how to write is to *write*. You can read about these skills, talk about them, watch films about them, and discuss them all day long, but you won't learn the skill unless you do it. Unfortunately, practicing writing (like practicing an instrument) is not always fun, and so, many children give it only a half-hearted effort. You can help your child master the skill of writing by giving him writing experiences that are different and more personally meaningful than the mechanical lesson he sometimes must practice in the classroom.

Observe Details

You can improve your child's writing ability simply by improving his ability to observe details. The child who sits with pen in hand staring at a blank piece of paper while complaining, "I can't think of anything to write," hasn't learned to consider all the possibilities contained in every subject idea. Take, for example, the famous beginning-of-the-year compositon, "What I Did Over My Summer Vacation." Every September students all over America write:

> "I didn't do anything special over my summer vacation. The end."

The teacher asks a question, the students answer it, and then they go blank—there is no more to say. These children need help looking at the pieces of the whole. A three-paragraph composition can be put together easily about even the dullest of summers if a child thinks to divide a typical day into its three parts:

Paragraph 1: "Summer mornings are slow-moving." The writer can then describe a morning of watching TV, eating breakfast, and putting on summer clothing.

Paragraph 2: "In the afternoon I played with my brother."
The writer can mention a few of the games and/or activities
that he and his brother enjoyed, such as: swimming, bike
riding, fishing, shooting water pistols, throwing stones
in puddles, etc.

Paragraph 3: "I can go to bed later at night during the
summer."

In this last paragraph, the writer can mention a few of the
things that he did during his extra stay-up hours, such as:
eating ice cream, catching lightning bugs, sitting on the front
steps, etc.

This may not evolve into a high-quality piece of writing,
but it is a positive step away from the "nothing-happened"
kind of composition

To develop your child's ability to observe and recall details, make a habit of talking about what he sees, smells,
and feels. When you're stuck in a traffic jam, for instance,
ask your child what he sees. "A mess of cars," he might say.
Begin to push, "What else?" "That's all," he'll insist. Then
draw him into conversation about the kind of cars, the kind
of people in the cars, and the roadway itself. Ask him to
imagine what's causing the back-up. Where does he think
the yellow car ahead of you is headed? How does he feel
about the delay? What can you do to avoid this jam the next
time? In writing, these answers would make a wonderful
story that began simply with "a mess of cars."

Make Opportunities for Writing

To foster writing skills, a child should have daily opportunities to write. In the classroom, these opportunities are
limited because there are so many other lessons to be learned
each day, so many workbook exercises to be completed, and
only so many hours that teachers can devote to correcting
compositions. But at home, you can give unlimited opportunities.

To ensure daily writing, help your child incorporate journal writing into his schedule. Buy him a special notebook

that will be for journal entries only, and encourage your child to write in it every day. You can probably make this writing seem like a treat if you allow your child to stay up a little later each night to do it. (Journal writing takes less than five minutes a day.)

In the beginning all entries are usually very short. If you suggest that your child write about what happened in school that day, don't be surprised if the written response is the same as his usual verbal response: "Nothing." Help your child overcome his writer's block by asking specific questions like:

Who sat next to you at lunch today?
What did you eat?
Did you go outside for recess?
Was your teacher proud of your class today?

Given these kinds of cues, your child's expanding observation capabilities will eventually lead to longer and more detailed stories. If your child is just learning how to write a few words, let this journal be a place where he can practice his new words. You can then help him verbally put the words in sentences that describe his day. When children see the relationship between the words they write and the lives they live, writing them down becomes meaningful and fun.

Don't abort the spontaneity of this process with criticism or correction. In these journals, the grammar, spelling, and punctuation do not count. This is one place the novice writer can express himself through the written word without anyone "fixing" it for him.

Don't Emphasize "Correct" Over Content

Writing is a process that involves a combination of skills. First, a writer must have thoughts to express. Then he must know the alphabet and know how letters form words. He must also know how to put words together in structurally sound sentences, and he must know and follow prescribed rules of grammar, spelling, and punctuation. Whew! That's a lot of skills to put together. Obviously, they don't all come together at once. Each is learned at its own pace and then slowly combined with the others.

You can help your child build on one writing skill to advance to another in the same way you encouraged his speech development. Simply put, children learn to speak through imitation and trial and error. They gain the confidence to experiment with sounds and try new words and new combinations of words through your support and encouragement. At the first utterance of the sound "da," Mom and Dad smile, clap their hands, and encourage the baby to try again. "That's it!" they exclaim. " 'Daddy.' Say it again!" This same kind of enthusiastic response to writing would encourage children to try again and again, and this practice would slowly improve the quality of the writing. Instead, parents often react to writing with criticism.

"That's nice," Gail said to her son when he showed her the Father's Day card he made for his dad. "But you spelled this word wrong; your penmanship is sloppy, and you forgot a period." In this kind of non-school situation, Gail and all parents should make sure their praise of the thoughts and the effort exceed their criticism of mechanics. Use the same sense of intuition that told you you could not teach your child to talk through scoldings, ridicule, and negative-tone correction. When your child first said, "Me go," you knew not to respond with a remark like, "That's not how you should talk. Now say it right: 'I want to leave the room.' " In the same way, when your young child writes, "skol" for "school," smile and praise the effort without correcting it.

Encourage Editing and Rewriting

As your child learns more and more writing skills in school, you should see an improvement in the mechanics of the written form. If, however, your child continues to struggle with spelling, capitalization, and punctuation, then in addition to encouraging journal writings (which are never corrected or evaluated), teach your child how to edit and rewrite for accuracy.

Let's say, for example, that you've encouraged your child to write a letter to his favorite magazine. The first draft should be nothing more than a collection of thoughts without worry about the form. Then, when he has fully expressed his message, help him fix the mechanics. Encourage him to look at each sentence to ask and answer these three questions:

- Are there any words I'm not sure are spelled correctly? If so, help your child look them up in the dictionary. (If you're willing to help him, your child will be more likely to admit which words are probably misspelled.)
- Are capital letters in the right places?
- Does the sentence have proper punctuation?

When the letter is corrected to the best of your child's ability, give him a good piece of paper on which to rewrite the final copy.

Writing to put thoughts on paper, then editing to correct the mechanics, and then rewriting for the final copy is the same method that most professional writers use. Assure your child that thoughts don't usually come out of the mind in perfect grammatical structures. Teach him to get the thoughts out first, *then* to fix them up. And emphasize that most people find it difficult to do both at once.

Supply an Audience

Writing is a form of communication. Its usual purpose is to convey a message to another person. This purpose can become clouded in the classroom because the teacher is the only person who ever sees the child's writing. He or she sees it not as the receiver of a message, but as an instructor who corrects errors. Adults would be insulted if their written works were returned with red correction marks. It would be obvious that the reader missed the message and focused on the mistakes. Although many classroom lessons need to focus on writing mistakes, at home you can give your child appreciative audiences who will enjoy what he writes and who will give your child a *reason* to write intellectually and legibly.

Encourage your child to write to relatives and friends on a regular basis. Young children will enjoy writing notes to Mom or Dad that can be hidden under the bed pillow or taped to the bathroom mirror. Write thank-you notes for presents. Write postcards from vacation sites. Write to a neighbor or social friend. The telephone, pre-written greeting cards, and photographs are all time-saving ways to communicate, but they also limit your child's opportunities to write. Give him an appreciative audience and a reason, and he'll begin to understand why everyone learns how to write.

You can also make writing fun and purposeful by finding magazines that publish children's letters, poems, stories, and art work. Use these magazine markets to show your child how other children write, and then help him submit his own work. If he wants to send a picture, help him write the cover letter to accompany it. Seeing one's work published is a wonderful way to learn that other people appreciate skilled writing. A few popular magazines that regularly publish children's works follow. Ask your child's teacher and the local librarian to get you copies of these magazines and to recommend others.

Magazines That Accept Children's Letters, Stories, and Poems

Boys' Life
ages 8 and up

Cobblestone
ages 8 to 14

Cricket
ages 6 to 12

Highlights for Children
ages 5 to 12

National Geographic World
ages 8 and up

Odyssey
ages 8 to 12

Penny Power
ages 8 to 14

Ranger Rick
ages 5 to 12

Stone Soup
ages 5 to 12
(This magazine is written by the readers!)

Be a Role Model

Through your own exciting habits you can show your child that writing is not just a way to pass time in the classroom. Instead of using the phone to say "Happy Birthday" or "Thank you," send a hand-written card. Instead of relying only on photographs to show friends and relatives how beautiful/exotic/exciting your vacation place is, exercise your powers of observation and description by writing to them about it. When you have an opinion on a public issue, write a letter to the editor of a local newspaper. Whenever you have the opportunity to write—do it. And call attention to your writing by reading it aloud to your child. Ask his opinion about the contents. When appropriate, encourage him to add a few words of his own.

Projects That Make Writing Fun

• *Write Picture Stories*
 If your child is too young to write a story in paragraph form, he can still practice "writing" by drawing a sequence of pictures. Let's say, for example, he has just come home from the zoo. Encourage him to draw three pictures that describe what he saw there. When he's finished, ask him to "read" his zoo story. Through these pictures, he will learn that written symbols can convey a message. When possible, send his picture stories to friends or relatives. This will reinforce the idea of speaking through a written message.

- *Write a Book*

    As your child learns how to write, help him record his stories and experiences in a book of his own. You can buy blank paper journals for this purpose or you can simply staple together a few loose-leaf papers. These "books" are different from journal entries because your child will write a story with a beginning, a middle, and an end, rather than just random thoughts. After a vacation at the beach, for example, your child can write a non-fiction account of his adventures and then add color illustrations. Or, if your child has a flair for fiction, encourage him to place himself or his favorite superhero, cartoon character, or rock star into an exciting plot of mystery, intrigue, or adventure.

- *Find a Pen Pal*

    A pen pal provides a child with a limitless supply of writing opportunities. When your child receives a letter from a pen pal, there is an implied obligation to write back. A pen pal is also an interested audience who won't criticize writing mechanics and yet will give constant feedback.

    You can find your child a pen pal within your own family if he has a cousin or family friend of his same age who lives a distance away. (Anyone who lives within your visiting or toll-free phoning area will not serve your purpose.) You might also ask your child's teacher if he or she knows a teacher in another school district who would be able to recommend a student pen pal. Or, you can write to the following organization to obtain a computerized list of domestic or international pen pals who speak English and are looking for an American student to correspond with: World-wide Pen Friends, P.O. Box 6896, Thousand Oaks, California 91359 (1-805-373-5149).

- *Use the Typewriter or Computer*

    You can enhance any of the writing suggestions in this chapter if you have a typewriter or a computer with a word-processing program. The novelty of using a keyboard to compose a piece of written communication is often just the catalyst some children need to get them excited about writing. If your child avoids writing assignments because he has difficulty with the mechanics of handwriting or because he tires easily, it may be worth the cost and effort to buy him a second-hand typewriter of his own, a new typing ribbon, and lots of crisp white paper. With the proper tools, this reluctant writer may surprise you with reams of creative masterpieces—or maybe he'll just be more willing to do his homework. Either way, it will serve to get your child interested in writing.

Mathematics

Your child's math lessons will often involve rote memorization and routine drills. The basic skills of simple arithmetic (addition, subtraction, multiplication, and division) are sometimes best learned through this kind of repetition. You probably have your own recollections of trying to memorize the multiplication tables and of doing long-division problems over and over again. When your child's homework assignments call for this kind of drill work, help him by giving encouragement and assistance. Then when the drill work is finished, use the activities in this chapter (and others you think of yourself) to help your child learn how to apply these facts to his life, how to enjoy using numbers, and how to recognize the value of mathematical literacy.

The Grim Statistics

The statistics regarding our students' proficiency in mathematics and their attitudes toward the subject paint a grim picture for a future technologically rich world that will rely on an abundant supply of mathematicians. A recent study conducted by the Educational Testing Service found the proficiency levels of U.S. students, age 13 (judged by certain standardized tests), to be far below those of students in South Korea, Spain, Britain, and Ireland. This weak grasp of the subject may be why fewer than 1 percent of college freshmen in 1988 said they intended to major in math (compared with 4 percent 20 years ago). Various other studies have consistently found that although U.S. students seem to have a working knowledge of basic computation, they cannot apply these skills to manage real-life situations mathematically. The skills to do this involve problem-solving through word problems, estimation, graphing, and an understanding of probability and ratios.

Using Math at Home

In your home, you can help your child rise above and beyond the level of basic computation by encouraging him to "play" with math. Talk about numbers; observe how they are used every day of our lives in phone numbers, street addresses, buying and selling, weather reports, speed limits, locating radio and TV stations, cooking instructions, telling time, and sports reports. Talk out loud when you have an opportunity to manipulate numbers. You do this when you change a recipe to increase the quantity, or raise the thermostat to provide more heat, or step on the gas pedal to pass a slow-moving car.

You can also give your child the mathematical edge by fostering a positive attitude toward the subject. Very often parents discourage math competence with statements such as, "I never liked math myself." Or, "I always thought word problems were dumb. Who cares which train gets to the station first?" Or, "I don't think you really need to know this stuff because calculators and computers will do all the work for you once you get out of school." Or (worst of all), "Girls never do well in math. I've heard it has something to do with the way a girl's brain is structured." Make a concerted effort to show a high regard for the use of math. Encourage use of the calculator as a tool to be mastered, as a means to speed easy calculations, and as a tool for computation practice. Be especially supportive of a daughter's efforts to master mathematical concepts, because she may be getting the tacit message from her teachers that boys are somehow naturally better in this field. This belief has absolutely no basis in fact.

Math Games

The following games are just a few ways to help your child grasp mathematical concepts. You can also make up your own and use the books suggested at the end of this chapter to find additional ways to play with numbers.

Addition and Subtraction for Younger Children (5 to 8):

1. Play board games that use dice. Each time your child adds the numbers on the dice and then moves forward on the board, he is practicing addition. You can practice subtraction by stipulating that the spaces moved are determined by subtracting the smaller dice number from the larger one.
2. Use a calendar to keep track of family events. Your child will learn in an incidental way to add and subtract numbers as he looks forward to special occasions.
3. Playing cards offers innumerable ways to practice arithmetic skills. For example, deal each player three cards and instruct them to each take a turn drawing new cards from the deck until they are able to add numbers together that equal seven; or to subtract numbers that equal four.
4. An allowance or bank account can give a child opportunities for practicing addition when money is deposited, and subtraction when money is withdrawn.

Addition and Subtraction for Older Children (8 to 12):

1. While shopping, let your child use a calculator to add up your purchases. Compare his final tab to the total that rings up on the cash register. To practice subtraction, tell your child how much money you have with you and let him deduct from that total each item you purchase.
2. On car trips, have your child record the odometer reading at the start. Then record the reading at the end. Ask your child to figure out how far you have traveled.
3. When you buy new carpeting, or plan to wallpaper, or are doing outdoor landscaping, ask your child to help you

measure the area. Give him a ruler or a yardstick (rather than a long measuring tape) so he will have to add successive feet to arrive at the answer.

Multiplication and Division for Younger Children (5 to 8):

1. When your child and his friends ask for cookies, talk out loud and help him see how multiplication will help you decide how many cookies to take from the box or tin. "Let's see, the three of you want two cookies each? Well, 3 × 2 = 6 cookies all together." Practice division in the same way by presenting the 6 cookies and saying, "I have 6 cookies for the 3 of you to share. How many do each of you get?"

2. Show your child how addition/subtraction/multiplication/division are related by giving him 10 pennies. Ask him, "How many pennies will you have if I take away 5?" Answer: 10 − 5 = 5 or, 10 ÷ 2 = 5. Add 10 more pennies to the group. Ask, "How many pennies do you have?" Answer: 10 + 10 = 20 or, 10 × 2 = 20. (Your child may see that multiplication is a faster method than addition.)

Multiplication and Division for Older Children (8 to 12):

1. Play the traditional game of dominoes. Points are made when the exposed ends of the dominoes played add to 5 or a multiple of 5. You can, of course, change the game to play the multiples of whichever times table your child needs to practice.

2. When shopping for produce, ask your child to estimate how much 3 pounds of apples will cost if they are 49 cents a pound. (Teach him to round off the 49 cents to 50 cents to make estimations easier.)

3. Word games can be fun (especially at times when there's nothing else to do, like when you're stuck in traffic or standing on line at the store). A sample game is: If 16 wheels crossed the bridge, what might have crossed the bridge? Answer: 8 bicycles, or 2 bicycles and 3 cars, or 2 tricycles and 5 bicycles, and so on.

Fractions for Younger Children (5 to 8):

1. Let your child measure out ingredients for your recipes as you point out where it says one-third or one-half in the recipe and the corresponding markings on the measuring cup or spoons.
2. Determine halves, quarters, thirds, etc., when separating things during daily chores. For example, "Let's cut this banana in quarters so all four of you can have a piece." Or, "Let's divide this pile of laundry in half so both of us can carry a load upstairs."
3. Use a clock to explain fractions of time such as, "quarter-past three" or "half-past five."

Fractions for Older Children (8 to 12):

1. Before you go grocery shopping, ask your child to look through the refrigerator and cabinets to help you decide what you need to buy. Decide what fractions of items are on the shelves: one-half a loaf of bread, one-quarter pound of butter, a half-gallon of milk, one-third of a dozen eggs, etc.
2. Use information about your family to practice fractions. If your child is 8 and you are 40 years old, what fraction of your age is your child? (One-fifth.) Use fractions to compare ages, heights, weights, how far each can jump, or how many times each can skip rope. These won't always work out evenly, but that's okay because life is like that in mathematics.
3. Use your child's love of baseball cards to encourage him to work in fractions. For example, by using fractions he can figure out how many times at bat it took his favorite baseball player, on average, to get a home run. To do this, he can put the total number of home runs (as stated on the back of baseball cards) in the numerator, and then the total number of at bats in the denominator. Therefore, if a player has 32 home runs in a given year and 640 at bats in that year, your child would write the fraction 32/640; reduce this to 1/20 and discover that this player averaged a home run every 20 times at bat.

Estimation for Younger Children (5 to 8):

1. Make a habit of asking your child to "guess" how far away items are, or how long something is, or how much something weighs. Then check the accuracy of the estimation by actually measuring or weighing the distance or weight.

2. Talk aloud when you estimate. For example, as you wonder how much money you should bring to the movie theater, say, "Let's see, if each ticket is about $7.00 and there's three of us going, I guess I should bring at least $21.00."

3. Fill a small jar with jelly beans. Ask your child to guess how many are in the jar. A good estimate can be found by counting the number in the top layer and then multiplying that number by the approximate number of rows. Or, your child might weigh 20 jelly beans, weigh the jar of beans, and then calculate an approximate number. Give your child time to think of ways to arrive at estimations.

Estimation for Older Children (8 to 12):

1. Encourage your child to round numbers off mentally and then compute them for an estimate of an answer. If, for example, your child is asked to multiply 27×52, he can quickly round this to 30×50 and know that the answer is somewhere around 1500. (The habit of estimation will let him know that he pushed the wrong digits on the calculator when the answer to this problem comes out to be 90,000.)

2. Help your child learn how to estimate a relatively large number by first sampling a small amount. For example, ask your child to guess how tall your house is. If he knows each floor is about 10 feet tall and the building is 3 stories high, he can reasonably estimate 30 feet.

Word Problems:

1. Help your child apply his arithmetic computation skills to mathematical word problems by casting homework problems into a story setting. If, for example, a problem reads,

"3 + 7 + 6 = ?" tell your child a story about 3 children who went to the park and met 7 others playing on the baseball field. When these 10 children were then joined by 6 others, how many children were playing baseball?

2. Talk out loud when you are using numbers to solve everyday problems. For example, "If 5 tomato plants fill 1 row of my garden, how many plants should I buy to fill all 6 rows?"

3. Provide opportunities for your child to solve his own daily mathematical problems. If he wants to buy a toy that costs $5.00, for example, but he has only $1.50, don't immediately tell him how much more he needs; instead, encourage him to figure it out.

Working with Large Numbers

Astronomically high numbers are a part of modern life. A billion-dollar government budget, the 93 million miles to the sun, and the 1 trillion cells in the human body are the kind of numbers batted around each day in the news, yet most people can barely conceptualize what 1 million is. Help your child understand large numbers by putting them in a familiar frame of reference. The picture book *How Much Is a Million?* puts numbers in perspective with real-world examples. You can do the same, by asking your children things like, "How many hundreds in a million?" Or "How old do you think the oldest human being is?"[2]

Vocabulary

There are many mathematical terms that your child will need to know. You can help him fully understand the concepts of these terms by using them in your conversations at home. When giving directions, for example, explain how one street runs "parallel" to another, while another is "perpendicular," and they all meet at the "intersection." Also, when you ask for the milk from the refrigerator, ask for the "quart" of milk. When you read from the newspaper the average temperature for this time of year, use the term "mean" temperature. Or when you are discussing the various ages of the kids on the football team, talk about the "range" of ages. As your child is introduced to mathematical terms in his school assignments, make an effort to incorporate them into family discussions.

Kids get turned off to math when they find it boring or irrelevant to their lives. You can help your child find numbers fascinating and make routine class assignments personally useful and meaningful by taking note of what they are learning in school. Then find ways to apply these facts to their hobbies, interests, sports, and daily lives.

Science

Science doesn't fit into a textbook. It belongs out in the world, all around us. Take your child's science homework lessons, combine them with the higher-level thinking activities (explained in Chapter 3) and show him how his world works. Let science exploration teach him about the nature of cause and effect, about the mysteries uncovered through close observation, the importance of classification to the order of life, and about the scientific process of problem solving.

You can do these things at home without teaching him "facts." It's better, easier, and certainly more fun to structure learning situations that will help your child make discoveries on his own. (This is especially wise since most of us don't know the answers to many scientific questions.) Science lessons are waiting to be uncovered wherever you are—in the city, suburbs, or farms; in a park, backyard, or kitchen; or on a beach or street. They cry out every time your child says, "How come the flashlight won't work anymore?" "Why is that plant dying?" "Where did all the dinosaurs go?"

Young children are naturally curious, full of wonder, and a source of ceaseless questions. But too often older children stop wondering and stop asking questions. It's not that they now have the answers; it's probably that their "why?" questions were all too often answered with an abrupt "Beats me." Encourage your children to keep wondering, and nurture a love of science by illustrating their classroom lessons through hands-on fun. When the answer to your child's question is an honest, "I don't know," lead him to the best place to find out. Don't expect him to be satisfied or encouraged with an "I don't know" that ends the discussion.

Foster Curiosity

Children are natural scientists. They want to know how things work, how they break, how they roll, how they bounce, how they feel and smell. Unfortunately, sometimes this need to know can be messy and inconvenient, so we tend to respond with an automatic "Don't do that." When a child bends down to feel the morning dew on the wet grass, we worry, "You'll get all wet." When he throws rocks in the pond to watch the expanding circles formed by the displacement of water, we yell, "Cut that out. You're going to fall in." Of course, common sense dictates that mud puddles are not best explored while walking to church on Sunday, but there are many other times when mud puddles should be experienced, felt, handled, and enjoyed—even though the process is messy. Next time, before you yell "Don't!" stop and think. If the circumstance is not dangerous, let your child enjoy himself and explore the science that's all around him.

Encourage Questioning

The goal in science is rarely to uncover a fact, give it a name, and move on to something else. Encourage your child to look deeper and to dig for more answers when he happens upon a scientific occurrence. You can do this by molding and encouraging the habit of critical questioning. Let's say, for example, that you see a bird in your yard and you call your child's attention to the blue jay. Your child looks, says "Oh yeah," and turns back to what he was doing. Continue your wondering and try to draw him into a discussion: "I wonder what the bird is going to do with the grass he's carrying in his beak? Oh look, he's building a nest. I wonder how he keeps the nest from falling apart? I wonder how long it takes to build a nest? I wonder if the female and the male share the work?" Finding the answers to these kinds of questions is not as important as asking them and developing the habit of wondering, questioning, and finding fascination in the world around you.

Experience Science

You won't have easy access to real-life examples of every science lesson your child brings home. But very often you can find a way to let him "experience" the facts. This is fun at any time, but especially important if your child seems to be bored or confused by a lesson. For example, let's say your child says to you that he hates learning about different kinds of rocks. You might listen to his complaints, encourage him to persevere, and quietly plan to find someplace where the two of you can go rock digging. Look for local areas of construction, along river banks and hiking trails, and even in your own backyard. Then challenge him to see if what his book says about different kinds of rocks is really true. Get a shovel, a bucket, some old clothes, and you're off. Finding the rocks and then handling, cleaning, classifying, organizing, and labeling them will certainly help him learn his school lesson, and it will also take away the "boring" stigma that he has begun to attach to science.

Make a habit of using the community resources that are available in your town or city. Ask the librarian to help you locate an area museum, nature center, planetarium, zoo, etc. You can use these resources to enhance your child's school lessons, to broaden his base of experiences, or any time the two of you just want to do something special together.

Experiments

There are innumerable science experiments that you and your child can perform at home. The following three are presented just to give you an idea of how easy and fun at-home scientific exploration can be. Following these experiments, you will find a list of inexpensive tools that you might keep on hand to encourage your child to explore on his own. Be sure to ask your child's teacher if there are any hands-on activities you can do at home to enhance the classroom lessons. And then head to your local library. In addition to the books suggested at the end of this section, the shelves are sure to be filled with books of scientific experiments.

Nature:

To encourage your children's interest in science, help them "adopt" a local tree, collect its leaves in every season, make a rubbing of its bark, draw its shape and note key events—such as the first color change in fall and the appearance of buds in winter and blossoms in spring.[3]

Light:

Light travels through water differently than it does through air. To show this phenomenon to your child, place a straw in a glass of water. Bend down so you can see the water line at eye level. Do you see something that looks funny? The straw will look like it is bent. Ask your child if he thinks it has really changed its shape. Let him guess why and how this happens. (Water breaks the path of light.)[4]

Forced Air:

You can show your child the power of air and let him have fun in the pool or tub at the same time. Cut an empty milk carton in half lengthwise. Put a hole in the bottom of one of the halves. Pull the neck of a balloon through the hole, and then blow up the balloon, holding the end tightly when you're finished. Place the carton and the expanded balloon on the water's surface and let go of the balloon's end. The force of the air rushing out of the balloon will push the "boat" across the water.[5]

The Tools of Science

A commercial chemistry set and microscope certainly encourage scientific exploration. But there are many other tools of science that you can gather together at little expense. These include items such as:

- binoculars
- a bug jar (an empty jelly jar)
- compass
- flashlight
- magnets
- measuring tape
- mirror
- plant seeds
- string
- tape

When you take your child outside with this kind of scientific equipment, you can guide him in specific lessons or just let him loose to experiment and explore on his own. Either way, the world around you is the best place to find science lessons that will supplement your child's classwork and instill in him the love of science.

It is estimated that by the year 2000, the U.S. will need between 450,000 and 750,000 more chemists, biologists, physicists, and engineers than it is expected to produce. In fact, a recent article in *Time* magazine stated, "The science deficit threatens America's prosperity and possibly even its national security."[6] Knowing this, thirty-six states since 1980 have raised their science requirements for high school graduation. Students are now getting a more in-depth view of the sciences—but are they enjoying it? Will they go on to make science a career choice? If you show your child the fun and the useful application of everyday science, he will certainly find his class lessons more relevant and interesting— you may also be providing for the future needs of this country.

Resource List

Reading

Write

- International Reading Association
  800 Barksdale Road
  PO Box 8139
  Newark, Delaware 19714
  Ask for a free copy of "You Can Encourage Your Child to Read."
- Child Study Children's Book Committee
  Bank Street College
  610 W. 112th Street
  New York, New York 10025
  Send $4.00 for a copy of their yearly Children's Books of the Year, an annotated list of the best new books each year.
- The National PTA
  700 N. Rush Street
  Chicago, Illinois 60611
  Ask for a free copy of the pamphlet, "Help Your Child Become a Good Reader."
- The Children's Book Council
  67 Irving Place
  New York, New York 10003
  Ask for the free pamphlet, "Choosing a Child's Book."

Books

- *A Parent's Guide to Children's Reading*
  Nancy Larrich
  5th revised edition
  Westminster John Knox, 1983.
- *Choosing Books for Kids*
  Oppenheim, Brenner and Boegehold
  Ballantine Books, 1986.

- *The Read-Aloud Handbook*
  Jim Trelease
  Penguin, 1982
- *From Wonder to Wisdom: Using Stories to Help Children Grow*
  Charles A. Smith
  New American Library, 1989

Video Cassette

- *On the Wings of Books*
  Cleary Connection
  Ages: birth to 3rd grade
  This how-to video helps parents instill a love of reading in their children. To order, call 1-800-513-6035. ($39.95)

Writing

Write

- Information Services, National Council of Teachers of English
  1111 Kenyon Road
  Urbana, Illinois 61801
  Send a stamped, self-addressed envelope for the free pamphlet, "How to Help Your Child Become a Better Writer."
- Consumer Information Center
  Dept. RW
  Pueblo, Colorado 81009
  Send 50 cents for the pamphlet, "Help Your Child Learn to Write Well" (#458N).

Books

- *Write from the Start: Tapping Your Child's Natural Writing Ability*
  D. Grave and V. Stuart
  New American Library, 1987
- *The Craft of Children's Writing*
  Judith Newman
  Heinemann Educational Books, Inc., 1985

- *The Magic Pencil: Teaching Children Creative Writing*
  Eve Shelnutt
  Peachtree, 1988

Computer Software

- "Writer Rabbit"
  The Learning Company (1-800-852-2255)
  Ages: 7 to 10
  Apple II Series, IBM/Tandy and compatibles
  In six sequenced games, children join Writer Rabbit at a
  sentence party and learn to create complete sentences and
  stories.
- "Sticky Bear Reading Comprehension"
  Weekly Reader Software 1-800-327-1473
  Grade levels: 3rd to 5th
  Apple, Commodore 64, IBM and compatibles
  This program includes thirty high-interest stories with com-
  prehension questions. Users can also develop their own stories.
- "Snoopy Writer"
  Random House Media 1-800-638-6460
  Grade levels: 1st to 6th
  Apple
  Guides beginning writer through each step of writing, edit-
  ing, and printing.

Mathematics

Write

- National Council of Teachers of Mathematics
  1906 Association Drive
  Reston, Virginia 22901
  Ask for a free copy of "How to Be the PLUS in Your
  Child's Mathematics Education."
- Consumer Information Center
  Dept. RW
  Pueblo, Colorado 81009
  Send 50 cents for the booklet "Help Your Child Learn Math"
  (#457N).

Magazines

- *Dynamath*
  Grades 5–6; $9.90
  Scholastic Inc.
  PO Box 644
  Lynnhurst, New Jersey 07071
- *Scholastic Math*
  Grades 7–9; $10.50
  Scholastic Inc.
  PO Box 644
  Lynnhurst, New Jersey 07071

Books

- *How Much Is a Million?*
  David Schwartz and Steven Kellog
  Scholastic, Inc., 1986
- *The I Hate Mathematics! Book*
  Marilyn Burns
  Little, Brown, & Co., 1975
  Grades 5 and up
- *Math for Smarty Pants*
  Marilyn Burns
  Little, Brown, & Co. 1982
  Grades 7 and up

Video Cassettes

- *In Search of the Missing Numbers*
  Davidson (1-800-545-7677)
  Ages: 6 to 9
  This cassette, which focuses on addition and subtraction, won the New York International Film and Video Festival Award.
- *Math Rock Countdown*
  Davidson (1-800-545-7677)
  Ages: 9 to 12
  This cassette uses a game show format to practice multiplication and division skills.

Computer Software

- *Math Rabbit*
  The Learning Company (1-800-852-2255)
  Four games help children learn to add and subtract.
  Ages: 4 to 7
  Apple II series, IBM/Tandy and compatibles
- *Math 1: The Mechanics of Word Problems*
  Decision Development Corporation
  Grade levels: 3rd to 6th
  Apple, IBM and compatibles
  Combinations of words and numbers through 12 are randomly displayed to present an almost infinite number of word problems.
- *Math 2: Building on Word Problems*
  Decision Development Corporation
  Grade levels: 5th to 8th
  Apple, IBM and compatibles
  This program presents arithmetic word problems using numbers 1 through 9,999,999.
- *Fractions One*
  Vision Software (1-800-776-6781)
  Grade levels: 4th to 8th
  Commodore 64, 128
  This program shows children the difference between numerators and denominators in a simple, clear-cut way.
- *Math Word Problems*
  Weekly Reader Software (1-800-327-1473)
  Grade levels: 3rd to 6th
  Apple, IBM and compatibles
  This program allows you to select and adjust word problems in addition, subtraction, multiplication and division to match student progress.

Science

Write

- American Association for the Advancement of Science
  Office of Opportunities in Science
  1333 H Street N.W.
  Washington, D.C. 20005
  Ask for a free copy of "Career Opportunities in Science."
- Association of Science Technology Centers
  1413 K Street N.W., 10th floor
  Washington, D.C. 20013
  Ask for the location of the science museum nearest you.

Magazines

- *The Electric Company Magazine*
  ($10.95)
  200 Watt Street
  PO Box 51177
  Boulder, Colorado 80321
- *3-2-1 Contact*
  ($11.95)
  PO Box 51177
  Boulder, Colorado 80321
- *World*
  Dept. 01085
  National Geographic Society
  17th and M Streets, N.W.
  Washington, DC 20036
- *Nature Scope*
  National Wildlife Foundation
  8925 Leesburg Pike
  Vienna, VA
- *Odyssey: The Young Peoples' Magazine for Astro Media*
  1087 N. 7th Street
  Milwaukee, WI 53233

Books

- A series of educational books by science writer Vicki Cobb
  is full of simple experiments that can be conducted with

common household objects. For kindergartners through third graders: *Fuzz Does It!*, *Gobs of Goo*, and *Lots of Rot*. For students in the fourth through eighth grades: *Magic . . . Naturally*, *Science Experiments You Can Eat*, *The Secret Life of Hardware*, and *The Secret Life of School Supplies* (Harper and Row). If your library doesn't carry them, call the publisher's hot line: 1-800-638-3030.

Video Cassettes

- *Romper Room-Volume 7, Explore Nature*
  Playhouse Home Video (catalog #6758) VHS or BETA
- *Conquests of Space*
  Jeito Concepts Inc. (catalog #8500) VHS or BETA
  A fascinating documentary incorporating film footage from NASA and other institutes that recalls some of man's greatest achievements in space.
- *Life on Earth*
  Warner Home Video (catalog #11710) VHS or BETA
  This acclaimed series was originally seen on Public Broadcasting Service. It is a fascinating history of nature that captures the mysteries of the earth. It took David Attenborough and his crew three years to capture this footage. (1986)
- *Dinosaur*
  Vestron Video (catalog #1087) VHS or BETA
  This Emmy-winning family TV show examines these prehistoric creatures and re-creates their environment through state-of-the-art stop-motion animation. It is hosted by Christopher Reeve.

Computer Software

- *Science 1: The Environment*
  Decision Development Corporation
  Grade levels: 4th to 6th
  Apple, IBM and compatibles
  This program explores the basic concepts of ecology.
- *Science 4: Understanding Our Solar System*
  Decision Development Corporation
  Grade levels: 4th to 6th
  Apple, IBM and compatibles

A simulation of space exploration to the planets provides the medium in this program for demonstrating and practicing the scientific method.

• *Accu-Weather Forecaster*
IBM
Grade levels: 3rd to adult
IBM (requires 512k and modem)
This program uses a modem to access current weather information from Accu-Weather. This information can be displayed in a variety of maps, graphs, charts and forecasts.

10

"Why do I need special attention?"

Identifying and Working with the Gifted and Talented, the Underachiever, and the Learning Disabled

All children are special; all are gifted in some areas, disabled in others, and underachieve in still others. But when a child's learning capabilities are continually off the average-student track, he probably needs special education programs in addition to the standard curriculum to enable him to meet his full potential. This chapter will give you an overview of the education of, and the parent's role in teaching the gifted and talented, the underachiever, and the learning disabled. If your child falls into one of these categories, use the Resource List at the end of this chapter to gain more information about your child's special needs.

Gifted and Talented Children

Lorraine always knew her son, Matt, was a smart boy. He had learned to walk and to talk at a very early age, and then later in school he earned exceptionally good grades. But when Matt came home from school with a paper officially labeling him as "gifted," Lorraine and her husband were surprised and confused. "We're not exactly sure what 'gifted' means," Lorraine confessed as she stood in the school library with other parents of gifted children. When the meeting began, it was obvious that many of the parents had unanswered questions, such as: "How smart are our kids?" "How were they identified?" "What kind of special program do they need?" "How should we treat them at home?"

These parents were venturing into the world of education for the gifted and talented—a place none of them had ever been before. Although gifted and talented (G&T) children have always existed, it was not until 1972 that the Office of Gifted and Talented was established within the U.S. Office of Education. Since that time nearly every state in the country has built some kind of program for the gifted and talented, and national spending for G&T programs has risen from $5 million yearly in the 1970s to $180 million today.

If your child is gifted or talented, he is among the 2 to 5 million school children who fall into this category. Fortunately for him, you are aware of his special abilities and by reading this chapter are seeking the information that will help you ensure that his needs are recognized and met. This will keep him from languishing among the 40 to 60 percent of the gifted population who are never identified.

What Is Giftedness?

"Giftedness" is not a trait that is easily or succinctly defined. The definition used by most American school districts comes from the U.S. Office of Education. It states:

Gifted children shall be defined as those children who consistently excel or show the potential to consistently excel above the average in one or more of the following areas of human endeavor to the extent they need and can profit from specially planned educational services:

1. *General Intellectual Ability*. The child possessing general intellectual ability is consistently superior to other children in the school to the extent that he needs and can profit from specially planned educational services beyond those normally provided by the standard school program.
2. *Specific Academic Aptitude*. The child possessing a specific academic aptitude is that child who has an aptitude in a specific subject area that is consistently superior to the

aptitudes of other children in the school to the extent that he needs and can profit from specially planned educational services beyond those normally provided by the standard school program.

3. *Creative Thinking.* The creative thinking child is that child who consistently engages in divergent thinking that results in unconventional responses to conventional tasks to the extent that he needs and can profit from specially planned educational services, beyond those normally provided by the standard school program.

4. *Leadership Ability.* The child possessing leadership ability is that child who not only assumes leadership roles, but also is accepted by others as a leader to the extent that he needs and can profit from specially planned educational services beyond those normally provided by the standard school program.

5. *Visual and Performing Arts Ability.* The child possessing visual and performing arts ability is that child who, by his consistently outstanding aesthetic production in graphic arts, sculpture, music, or dance, needs and can profit from specially planned educational services beyond those normally provided by the standard school program.

6. *Psychomotor Ability.* The child possessing psychomotor ability is that child who consistently displays mechanical skills or athletic ability so superior to that of other children in the school that he needs and can profit from specially planned educational services beyond those normally provided by the standard school program.

This broad view of giftedness is an improvement over a prior definition, which applied the title of gifted only to children with IQs of 130 or higher. Today's broader definition recognizes not only academic giftedness but other kinds of special talents as well. This expanded view complements the idea of multiple intelligence explained in Chapter 2.

Who Are the Gifted Children?

No one can hand you a list of traits that point directly to giftedness. Each gifted child, like all other children, is a one-of-a-kind being, with unique abilities, personality, physical characteristics, and needs. However, the following list of traits commonly found in gifted and talented children will give you some insight into what separates gifted students from their classmates.

1. *Heightened perceptual skills:* Child is acutely aware of and responsive to his or her environment; uses all senses, is keenly observant and highly alert.
2. *Intense curiosity:* Child probes for answers—through verbal questioning, by exploring independently, and/or by manipulating objects.
3. *Advanced problem-solving ability and conceptualization:* Child thinks logically, draws conclusions, makes generalizations, transfers concept to new settings, makes good educated guesses.
4. *Motivation and perseverance:* Child has an unusual degree of commitment to tasks (especially self-selected activities), becomes absorbed in work, puts tremendous energy and time into specific topics of interest, tirelessly pursues interest to point of satisfaction. (These traits may be manifested in hobbies or collections.)
5. *Drive to organize and perfect:* Child sets what may be impossibly high standards for self and for work, places great importance on quality of his performance.
6. *Search for challenge:* Child welcomes complexity (often selecting it over the simple), enjoys games of thought and reason (and resists being provided with the solution), plays with ideas and words.
7. *Originality and humor:* Child puts elements together in new ways, uses novel approaches to tasks and materials, often displays keen sense of humor, takes risks (often in the form of espousing unconventional or unpopular positions), is both flexible and fluent in generating ideas.
8. *Resourcefulness and independence:* Child seeks own direction, is self-initiating, has high tolerance for ambiguity.
9. *Fondness for elaboration:* Child loves to embellish by adding on to ideas, responses, and solutions; generates alternatives; is concerned with detail.
10. *Acute sensitivity:* Child reacts strongly to moral and social issues; feels joy, pain, injustice, sarcasm, rejection keenly; has intense empathy. (These abilities may make a gifted child painfully conscious of his separateness from others and highly self-critical. However, at the same time, these

very traits may contribute to the child's being well liked by peers and viewed by them as a leader. In other words, the social and emotional problems that may result from these traits may lie more in the student's self-image than in others' perceptions.)

Of course, *all* children exhibit some of these traits at one time or another. The gifted aspect emerges only when a child displays several of these traits to an exceptional degree. When this happens, it's a signal that the child may have special abilities and that need attention.

Some gifted children are quite easy to recognize. They are the stereotypical, highly motivated, well-behaved, academically advanced, prize pupils. But there are many others who, although gifted, do not do well in school. In fact, it has been found that many students who fail in school do so *because* they are gifted. This may sound like a contradiction in terms, but gifted children often can be found among the depressed, the discipline problems, the class clowns, and the dropouts. They get lost in a system that fails to notice and attend to their special abilities. History gives us many examples of gifted people whose talents weren't immediately acknowledged. These include:

- Einstein, who was 4 years old before he could speak and 7 before he could read.
- F. W. Woolworth, who got a job in a dry goods store when he was 21, but who was not allowed to wait on customers because his employers thought he didn't have enough sense.
- Walt Disney, who was fired by a newspaper editor because he "didn't have any good ideas."
- Leo Tolstoy, who flunked ninth-grade algebra.
- Louis Pasteur, who was rated as mediocre in chemistry when he attended the Royal College.
- Winston Churchill, who failed the sixth grade.

Fortunately for our society, these gifted individuals persevered through their failures and made their historic and valuable contributions to society despite rough beginnings. But imagine how many others don't use their talents because their exceptional and creative abilities go unrecognized in school systems where conformity, rote memorization, and drill work are the norm. Gifted children need to be identified for their own self-fulfillment—as well as because they have the potential to improve the quality of life for all of us in the future.

Identification of Gifted Students

Not surprisingly, studies have shown that gifted children are often first and most effectively identified by their parents. Affirmative answers to the following kinds of questions will give you strong reason to suspect that your child is gifted and talented:

Did your child . . .

1. . . . walk and talk earlier than most children of similar age and sex?
2. . . . show a comparatively early interest in words?
3. . . . show an early interest in reading?
4. . . . show an early interest in clocks?
5. . . . show an early interest in numbers?

Does your child . . .

6. . . . have an exceptionally large vocabulary for his age?
7. . ✓. express curiosity about many things?
8. .✓. have more strength and stamina than other children of the same age and sex? . . . seem to need less sleep than you'd expect?
9. ✓. tend to associate with older children?
10. .✓. act as a leader among children of his own age?
11. .✓. have a good memory? .✓. have a good visual memory?
12. ✓. . show decided reasoning power?
13. . . . have a high capacity for planning and organization?
14. . . . relate information that has been gained in the past to new knowledge?
15. . . . show more interest in creative effort and new activities than in routine and repetitive tasks?
16. . . . try to excel in almost everything he does?

17. . . . concentrate on a single activity for a prolonged period without becoming bored?
18. . ✓ usually keep busy with a number of interests or hobbies?
19. . . . persist in his efforts in the face of unexpected difficulties?
20. . . . figure out his own solutions to problems?
21. . ✓ have a sense of humor that is advanced for his age?

If, after answering "Yes" to a majority of these questions, you believe that your child is gifted but has not been so identified by the school system, then it's time to take action. Talk with our child's teacher, with the principal, and with the school psychologist. If your school has a G&T program, request that your child be considered and tested for admission. (You may have to insist if your child doesn't outwardly appear to be a super-student.)

Before being admitted into a school's G&T program, gifted students will usually undergo a series of tests. IQ scores may be used to measure intellectual ability, along with standardized test results to mark achievement; tests of creativity, language development, and motor skills may also be administered. In addition, teacher recommendations and even peer evaluations may be solicited to complete the picture.

You should not stop your quest for an appropriate education if your child is not admitted to the school's G&T program, or if your school doesn't provide special education opportunities for the gifted. Investigate community resources. Get in touch with the education or psychology department of a nearby college or university. The faculty may do private testing and/or may have a G&T program of their own. They may also be able to refer you to a private gifted-child association in your area. If you can't get this information from the college, call your state or local psychological association; a representative can refer you to a psychologist in your area who can administer tests to verify your child's giftedness.

Don't believe those who say, "Gifted students don't need extra help because they're already smart." These students do need encouragement and specific educational methods to develop to their fullest potential. They don't need "extra" work that makes them feel penalized for being smart, but rather should have the opportunity to do daily assignments that encourage the use of higher-level thinking skills (as explained in Chapter 3), and skills that both challenge the child to strive for answers and offer the satisfaction of a difficult job well done. Your job as the parent of a gifted child is to make sure he is getting that encouragement in the classroom and to offer it also at home. Your child should have every advantage that will help him flourish in his specialness.

At Home with a Gifted Child

The size and quality of gifted programs vary dramatically from state to state and even from town to town. Whatever type of program your child becomes involved in, you, of all his instructors, have the best opportunity to nurture and guide his development from year to year.

All of the suggestions and activities presented in other chapters in this book are certainly appropriate for working with gifted children. Also, the following suggestions, found in the book *Guideposts for Parents of Gifted Children* (see Resource List), will help you foster healthy intellectual and emotional growth at home:

1. Try to maintain a healthy balance between the two extremes of over-structuring and abandoning your gifted child. Allow enough independence and privacy for your child to pursue his/her own activities and profit from his/her own mistakes, but be there when he/she needs you—to lend support, understanding, guidance, or simply (and perhaps most importantly) a sympathetic ear.
2. Remember that there's a fine line between pressure and challenge. Your child needs lots of intellectual stimulation and plenty of opportunities to stretch to fulfill his/her potential, but he/she also needs time off for having ordinary kinds of fun.
3. Avoid comparing your gifted child in an evaluative sense to his/her peers (brothers, sisters, classmates, neighbors'

children, other gifted children). Strive to understand and accept the strengths and weaknesses of each child and to value the uniqueness of each. Your respect for individuality will be contagious.

4. Remember that all children need to share in responsibilities (at home, in school, within the community) and to be held accountable for age-appropriate standards of behavior.

5. Don't bend so far over backwards to avoid "showing off" your gifted child that you forget to express your appreciation of and pride in his/her special abilities and achievements. Genuine praise and encouragement are essential to all children and need not be feared as causes for self-consciousness or elitism.

6. Work closely with your child's teacher, school administration, parent groups, and legislators in supporting programs that will assure high-quality, individualized education for all children.

7. Appreciate and respond to the special joys, needs, and problems that separate your gifted child from other children—and do the same with the joys, needs, and problems that he/she has in common with other children. Take each stage as it comes, and have fun.[1]

Matt's mom and dad now know what "gifted" means and are eager to foster and encourage their son's special talents. But Lorraine is also aware that her son is first and foremost a human being. At a recent meeting for the parents of the gifted she explained her philosophy of raising a gifted child:

> We have a son who has been labeled "gifted," and we will work with the educational system to recognize and to provide for his special needs. But we are really no different from other parents. We love Matt for his own sake, and not for his achievements. Whether he chooses to become a doctor, a lawyer, or an Indian chief, we want him to know that we will always support him and love him.

We agree. Gifted children are special because of their potential, but they are also children with child-like emotions, fears, and desires. Treasure the talents of your gifted child, challenge him to reach for the stars, but love him because he is your child and let him know that that alone is special.

Underachievers

"I know you can do better than this," scolded Sean's fifth-grade teacher as she returned his spelling test. "So what," Sean muttered as he shoved the D paper into his jacket pocket. "I hate school anyway." At home Sean threw the crumpled test paper onto the kitchen table. "You have to sign this," he said to his mother. "And don't say I can do better, because I can't!" he yelled over his shoulder as he slammed shut the door to his bedroom. Sean's mother knew he could do better because in the past he had been an excellent student. Now that he was barely passing, he refused to even talk about the problem. Lately it seems that every conversation in their household ends with Sean leaving the room while yelling, "Leave me alone. I'm doing the best I can." But his parents and teachers know that he is not.

Who Are the Underachievers?

Sean is an underachiever. This means that like millions of other children across the country, Sean is not performing up to his capabilities. This lack of school performance is generally judged on the basis of past performance as well as aptitude, achievement, and classroom test scores. Underachievers (who are twice as likely to be boys than girls) have average, above average, and even gifted abilities; they come from all socioeconomic backgrounds, and they have no physical or mental explanation for their lack of performance.

The underachiever does not conform to a ready-made image. Some are very shy; others are loud. Some are bossy rebels; others are timid followers. Some are lonely; others are outgoing and friendly. This variability makes underachievers difficult to spot in a crowded classroom, but teachers say that these students often do have some traits in common. They tend to act uninterested in academic subjects, are disinclined to study, give up easily, and, most obviously, earn grades that are below the standards set by their past performances, or by IQ and other aptitude tests.

Why Some Won't Try

The underachiever exemplifies the old adage, "You can lead a horse to water, but you can't make him drink." Parents and teachers can give these students guidance, materials, and opportunities to learn, but if they don't want to learn—they won't.

If your child is an underachiever you might want to take a back-door approach to the problem. Don't confront him with an ultimatum such as, "You'd better shape up and bring home a good report card." Instead, try to identify *why* he isn't performing up to par, work to fix that underlying conflict, and then encourage him to find a renewed interest in learning. The following section will give you a brief glimpse at the most common reasons for underachievement. Knowing why your child lacks motivation will help you to better understand his predicament, and make better use of the suggestions that follow for working with an underachieving child.

Academic Burnout—"I don't want to anymore."

Without a doubt, parental involvement is a vital component in successful and happy schooling. There is, however, a fine line between encouragement and pressure. In this age of the "superbaby" mentality, it is all too easy for parents to get caught up in pushing, and competing, and overloading a child's life. Children who strive relentlessly to meet their parents' high expectations often become so highly stressed that they exhibit physical signs such as headaches, stomach aches, fingernail biting, and insomnia. Then they burn out and become underachievers. Good grades and high achievement are admirable goals, but you should be wary of the price your child will pay if these goals are gained at the sacrifice of playfulness, imagination, relaxing unscheduled time, and a willingness to take risks even when the task may meet with failure.

Are You Pushing
Your Kids Too Hard?

The following quiz, developed by child-development specialist Michael K. Meyerhoff, EdD, will help you determine if you're putting too much emphasis on your child's achievements. Answer yes or no to the following questions:

_____ Are you easily alarmed if your child's achievements don't always surpass those of his or her peers?

_____ Do you constantly sacrifice time and energy from your own interests to accompany your child to special activities?

_____ Are you so concerned about quality time that you find it difficult to relax around your child?

_____ Do you routinely set up a structured agenda for your child's day rather than going with the flow?

_____ Are you more concerned about school curriculum than the personalities of your child's teachers?

_____ Would you be greatly upset and consider yourself a failure if your child was not accepted by a prestigious school or program?

_____ Do you routinely choose activities and materials for your child rather than letting the child select them?

_____ Do you constantly insist your child stick with a task long after he or she has lost interest in it?

_____ Do you become impatient if your child shows an inclination to simply practice abilities already acquired rather than strive to attempt new ones right away?

_____ Do you often have to struggle to get your child to sit still for a "learning session" because he or she wants to do something else instead?

_____ Does your child only seem to be seeking your approval instead of displaying genuine personal pride in his or her accomplishments?

_____ Do you only note whether or not your child came up with the "correct answer"—and disregard the process?

_____ Do you consider how your child gets along with others to be relatively unimportant as opposed to the child's academic standing?

_____ Do you immediately implement advice obtained from "experts" without discussing it with family and friends?

_____ Do you religiously follow one expert's philosophy instead of putting together your own plan or employing advice from several sources?

_____ Do you find yourself withholding affection until your child has accomplished a certain task or exhibited a certain skill?

_____ Does your child seem to be learning more but enjoying it less?

_____ Do you have a specific long-term strategy for your child's "success"?

_____ Are you reluctant to leave anything about your child's "success" to chance?

_____ Do you find your child often fails to meet your expectations?

_____ Do you find you are rarely pleasantly surprised by your child's accomplishments?

_____ Does your child seem afraid or anxious, rather than excited, about new experiences?

_____ Does your child become frustrated and upset if he or she can't master a new task in a short period of time?

_____ Do you get very upset if it seems your child has spent the "entire day doing nothing"?

_____ Do you feel that "experts" are more qualified than you to make decisions about your child's life?

Scoring: If you answered yes to more than five questions you may want to reevaluate the goals you have set for your child.

Low Expectations—"I don't have to."

Some children develop a laissez-faire view of schoolwork in imitation of their parents' attitudes. Children are quick to learn what's expected of them and they respond accordingly. The parent who underestimates a child's abilities is not likely to encourage hard work and effort. When the child recognizes that his family has limited aspirations for him, he'll set his sights low and settle back into complacency. But if his parents refuse to acknowledge an "I-can't" attitude and if they routinely set high standards that they know he can achieve (based on what they know about his IQ, as explained in Chapter 2, he will have ample reason to work up to his full potential.

Low expectation levels are also fostered in homes where parents are distracted with and absorbed in their own schedules and problems. In these homes, parents may not have the time or mental energy to express an interest in the child's school work. It is not surprising, then, that the child himself loses interest in trying to achieve. Initially most children want to please their parents and make them proud. If they can't do this, they'll soon stop trying.

Emotional Problems—"Who cares?"

Children may lose interest in school and their grades will drop if they have "more important" things on their minds; family problems, divorce, moving away, or a death in the family can take away a child's reasons to strive for success. A depressed child has little need or capacity for school work. A child whose parents are always fighting has little hope of making them proud. A child who feels abandoned might find pity and attention in self-deprecation. Many of these children find an escape route through daydreaming, drugs, or delinquency. Others find solace in the negative attention they gain when their grades begin to fall.

Marc, for example, had been a good student, but he lost interest in school when his parents separated. At first he was too worried and upset to keep his mind on his school-work. But then he found that when he brought home failing test grades and letters of complaint from his teachers, his mother would immediately put aside her own problems to yell at him and then call his father to tell him the bad news. Marc had found an easy way to get his mother's undivided attention and to get his parents talking to each other again. For Marc, poor school grades fed his need for pity and gave him the attention he needed.

If your child has reason to say "Who cares?" use the information in Chapter 1 to show him that *you* do.

Boredom—"This is dumb."

Many underachievers are bright children who have developed the art of getting by. They are genuinely bored by their classwork and school assignments. They avoid the frustration of boredom by avoiding any work they don't have to do. For children whose interests lie in higher-level academics or in creative or physical outlets such as music, art, sports, or youth group activities, school may seem no more than a waste of their time. This most frequently happens when teachers treat all students alike (even though research has shown us that what's right for some may be totally unnecessary and ineffective for others). The result is that the underachiever often gets lost within the very system that is responsible for his care.

Although boredom is in itself a common cause for underachievement, don't automatically assume that it is your child's problem just because he claims, "I'm bored." Children often use this phrase as a catch-all excuse. Do some digging to make sure the problem lies with the level of school work and not in some other aspect of the child's life.

Eleven-year-old Rachel had been a model student until this year. Now, claiming "School is so boring," she refuses to do homework, won't participate in class discussions, and ridicules students who do. At a recent parent conference, Rachel's mother told the teacher about Rachel's boredom problem and her feeling that perhaps Rachel would be more interested in her school work if she were given more advanced work. "I can certainly give Rachel individualized and challenging work," said her teacher. "But from what I've observed, I think that she has caught this 'boring' bug from her friend, Ellen." After some honest discussion, Rachel's mom could see that there certainly was a close connection between the time that school became boring and the time that Ellen moved into the neighborhood. Rachel wasn't bored with school; she was yielding (as so many 11-year-olds do) to peer pressure as discussed in the next section.

Peer Pressure—"I'm no nerd."

Some students will stop doing well in school if they believe that being smart isn't "cool." Boys sometimes do this so they don't stand out and can more easily be accepted as "one of the guys." Girls sometimes play dumb when they begin to search for ways to become more attractive to boys. (Unfortunately the dumb-blonde syndrome is still alive within our culture.)

Children need peer acceptance, and so you'll most likely lose the battle if you insist that they find new friends or change their attitude. Instead, encourage your child to get involved in extracurricular activities that attract the better students and help him learn to think for himself by fostering a stronger self-image (see page 214).

Fear of Failure—"I can't."

Although it may not be immediately obvious, some underachievers are very competitive. They want to win at everything they do and are afraid of losing. The only way they can continually "succeed" is to lower their sights and avoid top-level competition. But by dropping back in the academic race they often miss basic skills; then, an underachieving pattern develops, and they fall further and further behind until they are struggling in earnest just to keep up.

Now the pressure is off—everyone starts believing they "just can't do it."

Children commonly develop this fear of failure in one of two ways. Either their parents are overprotective and do everything for their children, robbing them of opportunities to experience failure as a natural part of being human. Or, they have parents who set very high and rigid standards (and often older siblings who have met these standards) and they opt not to try at all so as to reduce the risk of disappointing their parents by trying and failing.

If your child insists, "I can't," when you know he can, observe his actions outside the classroom. Watch him at play: Does he worry more about losing than playing? When he starts to lose does he try to change the rules or accuse others of cheating? If you ask him to do something on his own does he respond with an automatic "I can't"? If so, stop running interference and let him make mistakes; let him learn some things the hard way and learn that when he makes mistakes no one gets angry and life goes on. To do this successfully you have to set standards that allow for some risk-taking and mistakes, and even failure.

Jamie, for example, feels free to try anything. He'll take on extra credit assignments, volunteer to lead group projects, and he eagerly participates in class discussions. He knows that if he tries and makes a mistake (even if the whole thing falls apart), his parents will be supportive, not disappointed. Jamie's parents emphasize the importance of effort, and they expect him to try his best at all times. After that, whatever happens is a learning experience and is okay with them. For instance, when Jamie wanted to take apart and re-assemble an old radio, he knew that if he took it apart and then decided it was too difficult to even try to put it back together, his parents would be upset. If, however, he took it apart, tried his best to put it back together but failed, they would be delighted that he was curious enough to give it a try. Children learn by accepting challenges, so give your underachiever the freedom he needs to take risks and to make mistakes.

Poor Self-Image— "I'm not smart enough."

Some people who feel inadequate try harder, but an underachiever who feels this way doesn't try at all. Because this child sees himself as dumb, stupid, incapable, and a hopeless case, he figures, "What's the use in trying? I can't do it anyway." Children with a poor self-image believe they have no control over their lives; they often see themselves as helpless pawns who cannot really influence the environment or achieve success. In fact, failure becomes a way of proving that they are right about their inability to succeed. The end result of a poor self-image is an "I-can't-because-I'm-dumb" attitude.

A child who believes in himself will aim high and succeed in school and in life. Therefore, this book, from the first to the last page, has been written to help you build a parent/child relationship that will boost your child's sense of confidence and self-esteem. If you believe your child is underachieving because of a poor self-image, you'll have to start on the ground floor and work with your child to build a strong parent/child foundation. While you're doing this you can also build up your child's self-image by following these basic steps:

- Help your child find a sense of pride through activities that he enjoys, such as computers, music, sports, or even skateboarding.
- Reward his achievements—no matter how small.
- Find something good to say about his work before you discuss the problems.
- Don't compare him to other children. Compare his successes only to his past failures.
- Teach your child that he *can* do things right.

Teacher Trouble—"It's her fault."

"That teacher hates me."
"My teacher isn't fair."

"How can I pass a test if the teacher doesn't know how to teach?"

Your child may use one or all of these statements to blame his teacher for his poor performance in school. As an objective third party, it's your job to determine if your child is not achieving in school because, in fact, there is a problem with the teacher, or if the teacher is being used by your child as a scapegoat to mask other problems. If your child has a long history of complaining about his teachers, this year's teacher is probably not the real reason for his poor performance. But if your child has been a good student in the past and has rarely complained about his teachers until now, you'd be right to assume that the problem might lie with the teacher. Some children can't work up to their potential if they are frustrated by a personality conflict or by teaching methods that work against their natural learning style. (See Chapter 2 for more information on learning style.)

If you believe your child's learning needs are not being addressed by his teacher, schedule a conference to discuss the problem. Approach the situation without laying blame, but rather with the attitude that the child has a problem that can surely be solved if both parent and teacher work together. Chapter 8 explains how to get the most out of a parent/teacher conference.

At Home with an Underachiever

All children need motivation to help them work up to their full potential. Some develop internal motivation that keeps them going without the need for external rewards and incentives. But others, especially underachievers, need some kind of boost. Chapter 4 outlines a program of rewards and penalties that you can use to motivate your underachieving child. In addition, the following words of advice will help you and your child find the road back to successful and happy schooling:

- *Talk to your child:* Put aside the confused and demanding attitudes that may have dominated your past discussions and adopt a supportive and caring attitude. Tell your child that you understand that school can be difficult; then share some of your own school-related fears and failures. Let him know that you want him to do well in school but you also want him to be happy. Assure him of your unconditional love—no matter what grades appear on his report card.

- *Don't do too much for your child:* Some parents are enablers. They enable their children to remain complacent by doing everything for them. They organize the child's school materials and get the homework from the teacher. They show the child how to do everything and help him avoid facing difficulties. They remind the child when he forgets, and they do things for him that he is capable of doing for himself. By smothering their child with help, they stifle opportunities for him to experience and learn responsibility, perseverance, and occasional failure.

  Don't try to improve your child's grades by doing his work for him, and don't nag or continually remind him to study. Follow the suggestions in Chapter 5 that show you how to set down homework ground rules and how to establish a homework time and place; then step back. Let your child take the responsibility for his successes and failures while you work to uncover and deal with the reasons for his underachieving.

- *Get organized:* Some underachievers are disorganized. They pass through each day in a muddled mess of confusion that shows itself in statements such as, "I can't find it," "I forgot," "I didn't know it was due today," or "I thought I handed that in already." Sometimes the statements are trite attempts to cover up other reasons for not doing assigned work, but quite often you'll find the underachiever wallowing beneath a pile of disorganization.

  While you continue the detective work that will uncover the root of your child's poor performance in school, help him address the immediate problem of disorganization. Establish a daily home routine that gives him some order in his day. Many children *need* to know when they are expected home after school, when they will eat, when they must do homework, when they can watch TV, and when they will go to bed. Then help him organize his homework area. Set up a tidy place that lays out his papers, pens, pencils, books, ruler, etc., and place a wastebasket near by. Buy him an assignment pad and a wall calendar that will help him learn to keep track of his assignments. This change in routine and atmosphere may make it easier for your child to pay attention to his school work. If not, it will at least take away his "I lost it/forgot it/didn't know" excuse.

- *Don't let your child be held back a grade:* Although it may seem that your child has not grasped the basic concepts he needs to move ahead to the next grade level, do all you can to avoid retention. Being held back can further damage your child's self-image and serves only to aggravate the underachieving syndrome. Work with the teacher and school administrators to find another way to bring your child up to grade level. Ask if your child is eligible for remedial or supplementary help through the special education department of the school system. Suggest that a final decision on retention be reserved until your child finishes a summer school program or a tutoring program that may be sponsored by a local college (call the dean of the education department to get the details). You might also hire a private tutor who can help your child learn the skills he needs to pass the necessary tests and exams. (The one-on-one attention from an interested tutor can work wonders to give underachievers a renewed interest in school work.) It is very unlikely that an underachiever will begin to work up to his potential because he must repeat a grade level.

- *Be patient:* Chronic underachievers do not change their patterns of behavior overnight. When you begin to explore the reasons for the lack of performance and to institute steps to encourage confidence and a more positive attitude, expect to find a long, slow road ahead.

The Lopezes, for example, patiently tried a variety of things to help their son, Rick, work up to his ability level. They carefully scheduled his day so there was always time for school work; they instituted a reward system for good grades and progress reports; they encouraged him to join the town soccer team, and they praised all of his accomplishments. But after one full year of their trying to help him, Rick responded only with continued resistance, hostility, and temper outbursts. Fortunately, his parents didn't give up.

As Rick began his second year of underachieving, he became interested in dirt-bike racing. He saved his school-grade reward money to buy a new bike and helmet, and he joined a racing team. His parents could see at the first race that Rick was a skilled rider and, most importantly, that he showed a sense of enthusiasm and self-confidence. At that point, it was tempting for them to say, "If you don't do better in school, you can't continue to race." Instead, Rick's parents supported his interest in racing, bought him books and magazines on the subject, and asked his teacher to offer Rick math, reading, and writing assignments that related to his new-found interest. After two years of below-level achievement, Rick slowly began to show a renewed interest in his school work; soon his grades reflected his ability, and once again he felt good about himself.

Even if it takes a few years to bring your child out from under the weight of below-level achievement, it will be well worth the effort. Your child is counting on you not to give up.

Learning Disabled Children

Seven-year-old Scott feels awful. He went to school today determined to do his best work ever. He wanted to pass his spelling test and behave in class all day. But now he was headed home with yet another failing grade and a note from his teacher complaining about his behavior. "It's no use trying anymore," Scott grumbled to himself. "I'm just stupid and everybody hates me, and now Mom and Dad will be mad at me again. I guess they have a right to yell at me because I'm just no good."

Unfortunately for Scott, and for hundreds of thousands of children like him, his sense of self-worth and his relationship with his family has become entangled in a grading system that ignores his learning disability.

What Is a Learning Disability?

The people close to children like Scott with learning disabilities often ask questions like:

"Why does he read 'dab' for 'bad'?"

"How come she could read all of these words yesterday and can't read any of them today?"

"If he knows so much about the nature and use of electricity, why can't he add 2 + 2?"

"I know he's trying, so why can't he learn?"

In addition to these questions, you may sometimes ask yourself, "Is my child just plain dumb, or is something wrong with him?" Although children with learning disabilities are of average or above-average intelligence, are considered psychologically normal, and have normal hearing and sight, the answer to your question is: Yes, something *is* wrong. Recent research based on evidence produced by brain-scanning devices has found that children with learning disabilities have brains that are structured differently than their peers'. Medical researchers are now using this information to learn how this affects the way nerve endings send out and receive signals from the brain. However, until more is known, the bottom line is: Children with learning disabilities *are* different from their classmates and need different teaching methods and materials.

Unfortunately, learning disabled (LD) children are not readily recognized and their problems are not always easily diagnosed. Children with learning disabilities are often confused with underachievers because they are intelligent but can appear to be unmotivated, lazy, disorganized, distractible, and stubborn, and above all do not perform well in school. The difference between the two is that the underachiever *will not* do his best because he has a motivation problem, while the LD child has difficulties achieving because of a cognitive/perception disability. Learning disabled children are also sometimes confused with retarded children because both have tremendous difficulty accepting and processing information at the same pace and with the same accuracy as "normal" children. However, the difference between the two is that the mentally impaired child has below-average capabilities, while the LD child has average, above-average, and sometimes even gifted capabilities. These comparisons draw a picture of an intelligent child who has trouble learning and who is easily mistaken for other types of students. This makes them an enigma to themselves, their teachers, and their parents.

The term "learning disability" is difficult to define because it is an umbrella phrase that covers a variety of learning problems. Some of these problems include: minimal brain dysfunction, brain injury, dyslexia (reading difficulties), attention deficit disorder (ADD), perceptual handicap, language processing problems, neurological impairment, central nervous system dysfunction, hyperactivity, and sensory deprivation. Knowing that any definition of "learning disability" will be imprecise, the most frequently used definition comes from the U.S. Department of Health, Education, and Welfare. It states:

> Children with special learning disabilities exhibit a disorder in one or more of the basic psychological processes involved in understanding or in using spoken or written language. These may be manifested in disorders of listening, thinking, talking, reading, writing, spelling, or arithmetic. They include conditions which have been referred to as perceptual handicap, brain injury, minimal brain dysfunction, dyslexia, development aphasia, etc. They do not include learning problems which are due primarily to visual, hearing or motor handicaps, to mental retardation, emotional disturbance, or to environmental disadvantage.

Identification of Learning Disabilities

Although there are early signs of learning disabilities, two-thirds of all LD children are not diagnosed as such until they are between 8 and 11 years of age. This happens because too often teachers and pediatricians are not fully trained to identify LD children. And so, it's the child's parents who most often suspect a problem and request testing and diagnosis.

If you suspect your child has a learning disability, talk with your child's teacher, principal, and school psychologist. Public Law 94-142 guarantees your right to a free evaluation. The goal of this evaluation is to determine which learning skills your child can accomplish and which ones he cannot perform easily. Diagnosis of a child usually includes:

- A comprehensive interview that covers the family and health history of the child
- A series of tests that evaluate intellectual capacity, school achievement, attention span, coordination, and information and sensory processing
- A psychological profile that analyzes emotional problems that can affect learning

Once the evaluation is completed, be sure to ask for a thorough explanation of the written report. By law, the school must provide formulated instruction to children with learning disabilities. Special education teachers will develop an individualized educational program (IEP) that details the specifics of your child's daily instruction; it also sets down reasonable expectations that will be continually monitored and updated. Make sure this is all explained to you in detail.

Sometimes LD children need more help than they get from the special education teachers and their parents. This is especially true if the learning disabled child has a damaged ego that was battered during years of defeat and misunderstood failures. In these cases, the child and his family may become victims of the problem rather than directors of its course. It may be necessary to seek professional help, if your child has become totally unmanageable or depressed. You'll want to find a psychologist or counselor who is specially trained in working with LD children, so ask your school psychologist for a referral or check with your local Association for Children with Learning Disabilities (the address is listed at the end of this chapter).

While your child is undergoing evaluation and diagnosis, you will probably be wondering what causes some children to have learning disabilities. The answer is an unsatisfying "no one knows for sure." It is known that learning disabilities affect almost 12 percent of the public school population, that boys are affected more often than girls, that the problem sometimes runs in families, and that a variety of circumstances before, during, and after birth may contribute to the problem. But since the exact cause is impossible to pinpoint, there is nothing to be gained by placing blame, finding fault, or feeling guilty about a child's learning disability.

A Parent's Role in Helping a Learning Disabled Child

Your role in raising a child with learning disabilities can be divided into three "A's": awareness, acceptance, and action.

Awareness:

If your child is having trouble in school, don't ignore the problem and hope that he'll grow out of it. Closely observe his work habits, his attitude, his difficulties, and his successes. Read all you can about learning disabilities so you will understand your child and have a clear picture of what he needs and where he can get it. (See the suggested resources at the end of this chapter.) This knowledge will also make it possible for both of you to work together, rather than remain at odds with each other. Together you can identify the problem areas, discuss them, and plot out strategies to maximize strengths and adapt to weaknesses.

You don't need special training to guide an LD child through the educational system. What you do need to do is:

1) stay involved,
2) ask questions,
3) make sure that he has opportunities to maximize his strong points, and
4) let him know that you understand his difficulties and support his efforts.

Acceptance:

Understanding the problems faced by an LD child is sometimes easier than accepting the problem in your own child. Before reaching a point of acceptance most parents experience many different emotions. They look for causes; they blame the school system, the teachers, and the other parent; they try to deny the problem; they wonder what they did wrong; they get angry and sad and worried.

All of these reactions are normal, but in order to help an

LD child you must get past these feelings. You must be able to stand up and say, "So my child has learning disabilities— now what? What can I do to help him? How can I make him feel good about himself? How can I maximize his strengths and minimize his weaknesses?" When you can do this, you'll see your child not only as a struggling student, but as a whole person. Your child will feel your acceptance and that alone will help him accept the things that make him different from his friends.

Action:

Once you are aware of your child's learning disability and have accepted it, you're ready for action in your own home. The following three plans of action will get you started in the right direction. Be sure also to talk with your child's teacher to find out how you can support his classroom IEP.

1. *Provide for structure in your child's life.* The LD child is often disoriented in time and place. Help him compensate for this weakness by establishing a predictable daily routine, by keeping his work area neat and organized, and by carefully explaining and repeating the order of things so he can better grasp what comes first, next, and last.

2. *Build his self-image through consistent positive reinforcement.* Children with learning disabilities face daily disappointments; the world demands things they cannot deliver, and they become frustrated at every turn. No wonder these children don't feel good about themselves. Help your child improve his self-image by fostering interests that complement his strong points, reward and praise his successes, no matter how small or incomplete. Remind him (daily if you must) that he is intelligent and assure him that although he may need more time to learn things than other children, he can and will succeed.

3. *Set high yet realistic standards.* Don't cripple your child's chances of achieving his potential by lowering your level of expectations. If you want him to grow up to be self-sufficient, give him realistically high goals to aim for. Give him responsibilities around the house that you know he can meet and then insist that he does. Become familiar with the expectations stated on his IEP and work with his

teachers to make sure he meets those goals. Don't let your child use his limitations as an excuse for failure; teach him to use his strengths to find success.

As you strive to help your child reach his potential, you must keep in mind that you cannot eliminate the learning disability. Simply stated, your child has a different kind of mind; you cannot alter it. But also remember that with your support and encouragement he can learn to function—even thrive—despite the disability and grow into a confident, productive, and contributing member of our society.

The Future of a Learning Disabled Child

No one can say for sure what the future holds for an LD child (or any other child, for that matter). There is still a great deal to be learned about how the mind functions and adapts, and far too many variables to neatly map out far-reaching plans. You should know, however, that with your help, your LD child can most certainly grow to be an achiever. Maybe he won't excel in reading, or he will still have trouble spelling, but if he learns to capitalize on his areas of strength, there is no reason for him to enter the adult world wearing an LD label.

Dr. Hagin, known for her long-term studies of LD children, learned the truth of this statement in a study that followed the progress of 87 students for 20 years. She found that 47 of them completed college: 8 became engineers, 2 became lawyers, 2 went into real estate, 2 became art historians, 14 went into management, and 5 did clerical work. Among the others were a journalist, a copywriter, an accountant, several teachers, and a photographer. All became competent, fully functioning adults.[2] There are also a number of rather famous people who are known to have suffered from learning disabilities. They include: Leonardo Da Vinci; Harvey Cushing, brain surgeon; William James, psychologist; President Woodrow Wilson; Vice-President Nelson Rockefeller; General George S. Patton; Olympic athletes Bruce Jenner and Greg Louganis; and entertainers Cher,

Tom Cruise, and Whoopi Goldberg. All of these people overcame, compensated for, or learned to live with learning disabilities. With your help, so can your child.

Gifted, underachieving, and learning disabled children need special attention. They deserve an education that goes beyond the daily classroom lessons to meet their needs and to encourage them to reach their full potential. This chapter has presented a brief overview of these areas of education; the following resources can give you more in-depth information if you need it.

Resource List

The Gifted and Talented

Write

- Office of Gifted and Talented
  U.S. Office of Education
  PIP/RAD OERI
  555 New Jersey Avenue N.W.
  Washington, D.C. 20208
  1-202-357-6164

- The Association for the Gifted (TAG)
  Council on Exceptional Children
  1920 Association Drive
  Reston, Virginia 22901
  1-703-620-3660

- National Association for Gifted Children
  4175 Lovell Road, Suite 140
  Circle Pines, Minnesota 55014
  1-612-784-3475

Books

- *Enjoy Your Gifted Child*
  Carol Addison Takacs
  Syracuse University Press, 1986
- *Parents' Guide to Raising a Gifted Child*
  James Alvino
  Ballantine Books, 1985
- *The Gifted and Talented Programs that Work* ($9.95)
  Order from: National School Public Relations Association
  1801 N. Moore St.
  Arlington, VA 22209

The Underachiever

Write

- Boys Town
  Communications and Public Service
  Boys Town, Nebraska 68010
  Ask for a copy of the pamphlet "What to do if your child is
  an underachiever in school."
- The Institute for Motivational Development
  200 W. 22nd Street, Suite 235
  Lombard, Illinois 60148
  1-800-468-4680
  This institute offers literature and psychological services
  for families with underachievers.

Books

- *Underachievement Syndrome*
  Sylvia B. Rimm, Ph.D.
  Apple Publishing Co., 1986

The Learning Disabled

Write

- Association for Children with Learning Disabilities
  4156 Library Road
  Pittsburgh, Pennsylvania 15234

- The Orton Society
  8415 Bellona Lane
  Towson, Maryland 21204

Books

- *Learning Disabilities: A Family Affair*
  Betty B. Osman
  Warner Books, 1979
- *Learning Disability*
  Alan O. Ross
  McGraw-Hill Book Company, 1977
- *No Easy Answers: The Learning Disabled Child at Home and at School*
  Sally L. Smith
  Bantam Books, 1980
- *Smart Kids With School Problems: Things to Know and Ways to Help*
  Priscilla L. Vail
  New American Library, 1981

Computer Software

- Send for the free catalog "Special Education Software for Grades K-8" from:
  Cambridge Development Laboratory, Inc.
  214 Third Avenue
  Waltham, Massachusetts 02154
  1-800-637-0047 (in Massachusetts, 617-890-4640)

Epilogue

We believe (and hope we have shown you) that successful schooling is not measured only by grades on a report card. It is determined by the degree of enthusiasm and excitement that a child feels toward education in general. It's that sense of awe that a child feels when he first sees the colors in a prism. It's the surge of pride he feels when he first pays for his own purchase and knows how much change he should receive. It's the inner delight the budding scientist feels when he informs his mom while she's cooking that if she adds salt to the water it will boil sooner.

It is our hope that the information, advice, and activities in this book will help you help your child get the most out of his elementary-school years and develop a love of learning that will serve him well throughout his lifetime.

If you find sections of this book to be especially helpful, or want to share other ideas about education, please drop us a note. As our work with child psychology and education continues, we are anxious to know what you think. You can direct your letters to:

Dr. Charles E. Schaefer
Division of Psychological Services
Fairleigh Dickinson University
139 Temple Ave.
Hackensack, NJ 07601

Chapter Notes

Chapter One

1. National Commission on Excellence in Education, *An Open Letter to the American People: A Nation at Risk: The Imperative for Educational Reform, A Report to the Nation and the Secretary of Education*. Washington, D.C.: Government Printing Office, April 1983, p. 35.
2. Walker, D. A. *The IEA Six Subject Survey: An Empirical Study of Education in Twenty-One Countries*. New York: John Wiley and Sons, 1976.
3. Dave, R. H. "The identification and measurement of environmental process variables that are related to educational achievement." Unpublished Ph.D. dissertation, University of Chicago, 1963.
4. Miller, JoAnn, and Susan Seissman. *The Parents' Guide to Daycare*. New York: Bantam Books, Inc. 1986.
5. Schaefer, Charles and Theresa DiGeronimo. *Teach Your Child to Behave*. New York: New American Library, 1990.
6. "Helping Your Child at Home with Vocabulary." Academic Therapy Publications, 20 Commercial Blvd., Novato, CA 94947.
7. Seligman, M. E. P. *Helplessness: On Depression, Development, and Death*. San Francisco: W. H. Freeman, 1975.
8. Bandura, A. "Perceived self-efficacy: exercise of control through self-belief." *Annual Series of European Research in Behavior Therapy*, 1988, *2*, 27–59.
9. ———. *Social Foundations of Thought and Action: A Social Cognitive Theory*. Englewood Cliffs, NJ: Prentice-Hall, 1986.
10. Stevenson, H. W., S. Lee, and J. W. Stigler. "Mathematics Achievement of Chinese, Japanese, and American Children." *Science*, February 1986, *231*, 293–699.

Chapter Two

1. McCall, Robert. "Genes, IQ, and You." *Parents*. December 1988, *63*, 131.
2. Perlmutter, C. "Seven Ways to Be Smart." *Children*. April 1989, *3*, 34.
3. Gardner, Howard. *Frames of Mind: The Theory of Multiple Intelligences*. New York: Basic Books, 1983.
4. Meisgeier, Charles, and Connie Meisgeier. *A Parent's Guide to Type: Individual Differences at Home and in School*. Palo Alto, CA: Consulting Psychologists Press, 1989.
5. ————. *A Teacher's Guide to Type: A New Perspective on Individual Differences in the Classroom*. Palo Alto, CA: Consulting Psychologists Press, 1989.

Chapter Three

1. Healy, Jane M. *Your Child's Growing Mind: A Parent's Guide to Learning from Birth to Adolescence*. New York: Doubleday, 1987.
2. Trachtenberg, D. "Student tasks in text material: what cognitive skills do they tap?" *Peabody Journal of Education*, 1974, *52*, 1.
3. Olson, Robert W. *The Art of Creative Thinking*. New York: Harper and Row, 1980.
4. "Stretching Your Child's Mind." *School Success: Guiding Your Child to Learning* Series. The Hume Co., Inc., 1989.

Chapter Four

1. Dornbusch, Sanford M., Philip L. Ritter, P. Herbert Leiderman, Donald F. Roberts, and Michael J. Fraleigh. "The relation of parenting style to adolescent school performance." *Child Development*, 1987, *58*, 1244–1257.

2. Van Hecke, Madeleine, and Robert Tracy. "The influence of adult encouragement on children's persistence." *Child Study Journal*, 1987, *17*, 251–268.
3. Rogan, Ed. "Getting bucks for B's." *Children.* October 1988, *2*, 20.
4. Toufexis, Anastasia. "Report cards can hurt you." *Time.* May 1, 1989, *133*, 75.

Chapter Six

1. Rudman, Masha. "Your Child and Testing." *School Success: Guiding Your Child to Learning Series*. The Hume Company, Inc., 1989.

Chapter Seven

1. Weaver, Constance. *Psycholinguistics and Reading*. Cambridge, Massachusetts: Winthrop Publishers, 1980.
2. Robinson, Frank. *Effective Study*. New York: Harper and Row, 1946.
3. *School House Rock!* Golden Book Video. American Broadcasting Companies, 1987.
4. "Studying: A Key to Success . . . Ways Parents Can Help." International Reading Association, 800 Barksdale Road, Newark, Delaware 19714.

Chapter Nine

1. Sloan, Glenna. "Good Books Make Reading Fun for Your Child." International Reading Association, 800 Barksdale Road, Newark, Delaware 19714.
2. Schwartz, David. *How Much Is a Million?* New York: Scholastic Inc., 1986.

3. Mittenthal, Sue. "Help Your Child to Be a Better Student." *McCall's*. September 1984, 111:12, 64.
4. Carter, Beth. "Science Can Be Fun." *Parents*. June 1989, *64*, 137.
5. Wyler, Rose. *What Happens If . . . ?* New York: Walker Publication Co., 1974.
6. Tifft, Susan. "A Crisis Looms in Science." *Time*. September 11, 1989, *134*, 68.

Chapter Ten

1. Strang, Ruth. *Guideposts for Parents of Gifted Children.* New York: Bureau of Publications, Teachers College, Columbia University, 1958.
2. Blau, Melinda. "Learning the Hard Way." *New York*. September 26, 1988, *21*, 106.

Index